PREHISTORIC POTTERY IN CHINA

PREHISTORIC POTTERY IN CHINA

By

G. D. WU 吳金鼎

Ph.D. (London)

PUBLISHED ON BEHALF OF
THE COURTAULD INSTITUTE OF ART, UNIVERSITY OF LONDON

BY

KEGAN PAUL, TRENCH, TRUBNER & Co., Ltd.
Broadway House : Carter Lane, London, E.C.

First published 1938

PRINTED IN GREAT BRITAIN BY
STEPHEN AUSTIN AND SONS, LTD., HERTFORD.

CONTENTS

CONTENTS

N.B.—Works are quoted in the text according to their serial number.

LIST OF ILLUSTRATIONS

About half the illustrations are made from actual specimens, most of which belong to the Academia Sinica. The rest have been copied in line drawings or photographed from certain publications which are indicated in parentheses.

MAPS

xi

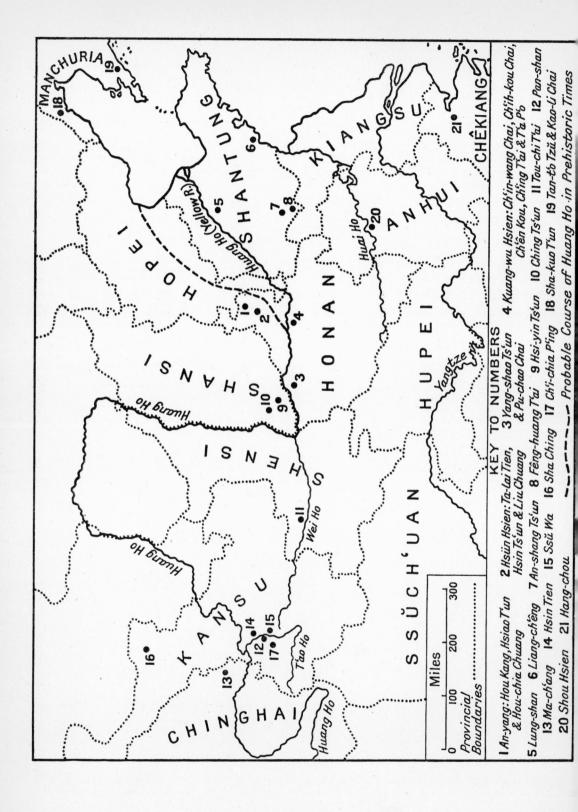

KEY TO NUMBERS

1 An-yang: Hou Kang, Hsiao T'un & Hou-chia Chuang 2 Hsün Hsien: Ta-lai Tien, Hsin Ts'un & Liu Chuang 3 Yang-shao Ts'un & Pu-chao Chai 4 Kuang-wu Hsien: Ch'in-wang Chai, Ch'ih-kou Chai, Chên Kou, Ching T'ai & Ta P'o

5 Lung-shan 6 Liang-chêng 7 An-shang Ts'un 8 Fêng-huang T'ai 9 Hsi-yin Ts'un 10 Ching Ts'un 11 Tou-chi Tai 12 Pan-shan

13 Ma-ch'ang 14 Hsin Tien 15 Ssŭ Wa 16 Sha Ching 17 Ch'i-chia P'ing 18 Sha-kuo Tun 19 Tan-tô Tzŭ & Kao-li Chai

20 Shou Hsien 21 Hang-chou

Provincial Boundaries ·········

- - - Probable Course of Huang Ho in Prehistoric Times

Part I

INTRODUCTION

PART I

INTRODUCTION

Section 1.—The term " Prehistoric " in the title of this thesis is meant to denote the time before the Shang-Yin dynasty, including all the pottery-making periods. It is not to be inferred that I share the views of modern sceptics who do not believe in the existence of the Hsia, the dynasty traditionally reputed to have preceded the Shang-Yin. My attitude is this : since archæologists have not yet found any undisputed evidence of the Hsia, it is reasonable to call Prehistoric the period before the historic Shang-Yin. Some may prefer to use the term " Proto-historic " for the legendary beginning of Chinese culture. But it is unsuitable for the scope of this thesis, as it covers a field which stretches too far back beyond the traditional dawn of Chinese history.

The territory concerned approximately corresponds to the northern part of present-day China. This area may be further divided into two regions, viz. the Plateau including Kansu, Shensi, Shansi, and a part of Western Honan, and the Plain including large parts of Hopei, Honan, and Shantung.

Section 2.—Pottery usually amounts to more than 90 per cent of the finds at any excavated dwelling site. In such circumstances, it is only natural that pottery should have been regarded as more important than the other artifacts. We must, however, keep in mind that earthenware pots are only one kind of ancient domestic utensil. On the one hand, we admit that the study of pottery may lead us to understand the general tendency of a cultural evolution, and possibly the relationship between cultures ; on the other, we must guard against making speculations without taking account of cultural remains other than pottery. There are the objects of stone,

3

bone, shell, and other materials, each of which deserves attention in the solution of archæological problems. As this thesis is devoted to pottery only, the reader must not be disappointed to find that certain topics in Chinese archæology are omitted, since they are beyond the proper scope of our study.

Some pottery finds are not discussed in this thesis, for instance, those of Dr. R. Torii and other Japanese scholars, and those of the Chinese scholar Mr. S. Y. Liang both in Manchuria and Mongolia, those of Father E. Licent in Northern Hopei, those of Mr. D. C. Graham at Hanchou in Ssǔch'uan, and those of Professor P. L. Yüan in Chinese Turkestan. The reason is either because the finds belong to historic periods and are beyond the scope of this thesis, or because they are inaccessible to me and are so briefly reported that they are of no value for my study. Some finds of the historic period, such as the Shang-Yin ware from Hsiao T'un, are briefly described in this thesis, because in the Third Part I try to show the general tendency of the development of the characteristics of prehistoric wares.

Section 3.—As to my methods, I have followed a very natural procedure. I have first studied the various pottery groups, then I have compared them. Further, I have tried to classify the wares, and finally I have constructed the chronological table. In the study of the various provincial groups I have paid attention to as many as seven characteristics of pottery, i.e. colour, shape, material, method of making, thickness, surface treatment, and decoration, because I believe that if many characteristics are studied, the result will be more accurate than if the study were limited to one or two.

I am of the opinion that ancient techniques can only be identified either by experiments or by comparison with modern parallels. Within certain limitations I have followed this principle. Experiments are justified by the fact that the function of the human hand must have been the same in ancient times as it is at the present day. By using the same tools the same result will be produced. The choice of modern parallels for comparison is also justified because the Chinese people, especially the farmers, are conservative and preserve to a remarkable degree the ancient ways. In many cases, a problem of technique may be solved by comparing the ancient relics with modern equivalents.

For the purpose of comparing I always kept in mind three principles : (1) to pay equal attention to distinctive peculiarities as well as to points of resemblance, (2) to pay equal attention to the various features of pottery, and (3) to give careful consideration to the two factors, time and space. My purpose in comparing objects distant in time or in space is to concentrate on technique. In order to arrive at a general classification of the prehistoric wares, I used the seven characteristics in order to build up a system. In constructing the chronological table I based my arguments not only on the evidence of pottery, but also on some other associated finds.

Section 4.—In 1927 I started my archæological explorations in the province of Shantung, and in the next year I discovered the Black Pottery culture there. In 1930 I joined the excavations of the Academia Sinica in Northern Honan. There I had the opportunity of studying more thoroughly the various kinds of ancient remains, especially pottery. Such studies have led me to take a profound interest in the ceramic art of ancient China, to which I have since devoted myself. In 1933, holding a scholarship from the Government of Shantung, I became a student in the University of London, my studies being directed by Professor W. Perceval Yetts. In 1935, with a grant from the Universities' China Committee, I went back to China and spent there a whole summer for the purpose of examining the new ceramic discoveries, especially those of the prehistoric period. My task was made easy by the kindness of friends and members of various learned institutions in China. The results of that visit have contributed largely to this thesis.

Section 5.—Before attempting a survey of the various pottery groups it seems fitting first of all to give a comprehensive account of the recent discoveries of prehistoric pottery at about fifteen important sites which have been explored up to the present day.

The most important discoveries of pottery in recent years may

5

be classified into two groups, the cultural group connected with the Red Pottery, which has been called " Yang-shao ", and the cultural group connected with the Black Pottery, which has been called " Lung-shan ". The Red Pottery was discovered in Honan in 1921 by Dr. J. G. Andersson. Many other sites of what he believed to be the same culture were found by him in Kansu in 1923–4. The details of his discoveries have already been published in his *Children of the Yellow Earth* (Bibl. 5), and I shall not repeat them here. All I need mention is that the discovery of the " Yang-shao " culture and the publications on this subject have been welcomed by Chinese students of ancient history with great interest. Within the last thirty years, they have often heard of foreign scholars exploring in China, and such names as Chavannes, Stein, Gründwedel, von Le Coq, Torii, and Kozlov are quite familiar to their ears. Reports of these explorations, though in various foreign languages, have been read with interest in the learned circles of that country. Dr. Andersson, who has his reports written both in English and Chinese, and published by a Chinese institution, has won the favour of the Chinese more than any other explorer. His influence and that of other foreign explorers on Chinese archæology can hardly be exaggerated, for we see that much attention is paid by Chinese scholars to new methods which are different from those which they have inherited from the Sung dynasty (A.D. 960–1277).

In the year 1926, between 5th February and 26th March, Dr. Li Chi, then Lecturer at the Tsing Hua University, Pei-p'ing, went on a joint trip with Professor P. L. Yüan to Southern Shansi, for the purpose of making an archæological survey of the valley of the River Fên. The results were published in the *Smithsonian Miscellaneous Collections, 1927* (Bibl. 12), from which I have derived my information. In the Fu-shan district, near the village of Chiao-t'ou Ho, he picked up a piece of red pottery with black painted designs. He soon found many other similar pieces in the same place and the main source was identified as a narrow strip of land quite near the village. Part of the cultural layer has been cut into by the road and is exposed.

6

Dr. Li collected from this exposed surface many sherds. This was the first prehistoric site found by Dr. Li in Shansi. The second one was discovered in Hsia Hsien, the traditional centre of the Hsia dynasty. This site is near the village of Hsi-yin, covering an extensive area. In October of the same year Dr. Li and Professor Yüan returned to the second site and started an excavation which lasted nearly six weeks. The finds filled more than sixty large packing cases, mostly pottery with a small proportion of implements of stone and other materials. Dr. Li's report was published in 1927 in Chinese (Bibl. 13), and that on the pottery by Mr. Liang Ssŭ-yung in 1930 in English (Bibl. 18).

When Dr. Li was excavating the prehistoric site at Hsi-yin, I was then studying at the Research Institute of the Tsing Hua University. Dr. Li brought back his finds to the University. The exhibition of the representative finds and the speeches made by Dr. Li and Professor Yüan at a public meeting of welcome succeeded in presenting the story in such a vivid and interesting way that I could not help thinking that I might one day find such a site, study it, excavate it, and write its history. When I had finished my studies in the summer of 1927, I accepted a position as an instructor in the Cheeloo University at Chi-nan, the capital of Shantung province. Like the other provinces in North China, Shantung is rich in antiquities, and it is no exaggeration to say that ancient remains prior to the Han dynasty (206 B.C.– A.D. 220) could be found in every Hsien, or district. Therefore, I was glad to have this opportunity to do archæological work in this University.

It became known to me then that there was an old city, P'ing-ling, about 25 miles east of modern Chi-nan. On 24th March, 1928, I went there for the purpose of an investigation, with a friend, Mr. H. D. Ts'uei, who was on his way to inspect a school at Lung-shan. At ten in the morning we arrived at Lung-shan, a big village 2 miles west of the old city. After a hasty breakfast we started our exploration with a school teacher, Mr. S. T. Chang, as guide. As we went out of the village we came to the bridge over the River

Wu-yüan, the east bank of which rose to a height of about 20 feet. A road had been cut through that bank. It was about 50 feet long and rose between two vertical walls to a high plain. When we reached the plain we saw a terrace immediately in front of us and a road cut through it in the same way. As we passed between the walls, I noticed an exposed stratum containing potsherds of a deep ashy colour. At that time I had been so much attracted by the old city toward which we were now making our way, that I was reluctant to stop even for a minute to examine the exposed remains. We passed this terrace hastily because the ruined walls of the old city stood right in front of us invitingly. After walking on for about half an hour, we arrived at an opening in the city wall which later I identified with the west gate of the city. It was there that we started our investigation and collection of ancient objects. We spent a happy day within the circle of the old walls, collecting various kinds of ancient objects, chiefly pottery, though nothing earlier than the Han was found, and the best of our finds were two coin-moulds of the *wu shu* type. This was the first exploration. On 4th May, I went to Lung-shan again ; this time Mr. Chang and I chose to go to the north of the village instead of the east, hoping to find something different there. As we got to the high bank of a ditch just north of the village, I happened to turn my face to the east, and saw again the terrace which we had passed in the last trip to the old city. Mr. Chang reminded me that it was the same terrace which we had seen before and that it was called O-ya Ch'êng, or " City of Geese and Ducks ". The ruined rampart around the terrace was still visible, and it seemed to me to hold out more promise of archæological discovery than the other sites. I told Mr. Chang that I would rather go back there instead of exploring to the north. So, with this objective we crossed the river, and came directly to the terrace. Confining my attention to the west wall of the terrace which contains a rich deposit of ancient remains, I started to dig and found potsherds, pieces of sea-shells, and bone implements. The primitive characteristics of those finds seemed to hint at the existence of stone tools, but so far I had not found any. Nor did I come upon tiles, bricks, coal-ash, which were all plentiful at P'ing-ling, the old city. That afternoon when I went to P'ing-ling again, I could not help comparing in my mind those two sites, P'ing-ling and the newly discovered one. Soon I formed the conclusion that the latter must be much earlier than P'ing-ling, which dates from the Han dynasty. I began to surmise that the new site might be that of prehistoric dwellings. Soon afterwards my archæological interest turned to the sphere of prehistoric culture, and I paid less attention to P'ing-ling and Han antiquities. At that time, owing to the lack of specimens for comparison and books for reference, I could not do much work with my finds. Gradually, however, I succeeded in formulating some sort of theory about this site, though I kept it to myself, not wishing to make it public until I had collected more evidence as to its early date.

One day in the summer of 1929, I managed to pay another visit to Lung-shan. All the finds which I made in the morning merely duplicated my former collection ; but in the afternoon, when I dug into the north-west corner of the terrace, I found unexpectedly a celt of basalt, well-made and polished. This was my first discovery of a stone tool, and it confirmed my hypothesis of the existence of stone tools at this site. This site, which was surveyed two years later, was found to cover an area of about 1,400 square feet, raised about 6–20 feet above the level of the surrounding fields. With the exception of part of the east side, all the other sides of the mound were either terraced, or steeply sloping. The cultural strata varied in depth with an average of about 9 feet. Above them there was an agricultural layer about 1 foot thick. The colour of the surface of the exposed strata was invariably dark yellow, but underneath we found the grey soil containing many potsherds, animal bones, shells, and fragments of stone implements. The colour of any cultural layer is, as a rule, ashy grey, but long exposure causes it to become yellow like the cultivated land. In some places I found big lumps of clay burnt red, possibly from ancient hearths or kilns. This time the thing that attracted my attention most was a kind of very thin, finely made black pottery. Since this particular ware was always associated with stone, bone, and shell implements, it was clear that it must belong to an early stage of culture. Between the summer and October of this year, I made three more visits, collecting specimens and studying the topographic features of the site. So far I had not found metals, tiles, or bricks, but all my finds could be classified as stone, bone, shell, and pottery artifacts.[1]

In the winter of 1929 I left the Cheeloo University and accepted a position in the National Research Institute of History and Philology, Academia Sinica, then in Pei-p'ing. In the autumn of 1930 I was sent to Lin-chih, a district in eastern Shantung, accompanied by Mr. D. C. Yü, for the purpose of an archæological investigation. One site I had to explore was that of the Ch'i capital of the Chou period. For a long time it has been famous for yielding antiquities and it has been a hunting ground for curio-seekers. At first I was so dazzled and perplexed by the great number of attractive materials lying exposed on the surface that for several days I collected only these Chou relics and did not look for remains of an earlier culture. But one day I found two fragments of stone tools and two fragments of black pottery of the same type as that of Lung-shan, and it suggested the idea that black pottery might not be limited to the one site. At all events, it could be found here at Lin-chih, about 60 miles east. After reading my report on the investigations at Lin-chih, Dr. Li Chi, the head of the Department of Archæology in the Academia Sinica, proposed to make a joint trip with me to Lin-chih. But I suggested to him that it might be worth while to make another investigation of the Lung-shan site first, and he agreed. It was on 18th October that Dr. Li went with me to see the Lung-shan site. Perhaps we may say that owing to this visit the Black Pottery culture was introduced to the scientific world. When we returned from this trip, Dr. Li assured me without any hesitation that this newly discovered site and its contents represented a unique culture the importance of which in prehistoric archæology can hardly be

[1] In 1930 I published an account of this discovery in Chinese, Bibl. 29.

exaggerated. Then I found that Dr. Li's impression of this site was absolutely in agreement with the theory which I had cherished in my mind for many years. All my hypotheses and inferences were then strengthened by the opinion of this experienced archæologist.

The Academia Sinica, co-operating with the Provincial Government of Shantung, subsequently, established a station at Chi-nan for archæological research, of which I was put in charge. As we began to make plans for the first excavation, Dr. Li urged strongly that the start should be made at the Black Pottery site near Lung-shan. After some consideration, we all agreed with him, and we carried out our work from 7th November to 8th December. This excavation showed that not only the Black Pottery and its associated objects represented a unique culture, but also—and this was beyond our expectations—that there existed a later stratum above the Black Pottery stratum. When the work was completed, Dr. Li, in his report to the Academia Sinica and the Government of Shantung, summarized the results in the following words :—

" Our intensive digging which lasted about a month has succeeded not only in achieving what we expected, but also in revealing the fact that there are at this site two layers of different cultural epochs. The upper layer contains relics of the Bronze Age and is surrounded by the remains of a mud wall ; the *tou* and the *li* seem to be peculiar to this culture. . . . The oracle bones in this layer are in some ways like those of Yin-hsü (Hsiao T'un). . . . The lower layer is neolithic. The finds consist mainly of Black Pottery with a small proportion of grey, red, and white ware. The stone tools may be classified into axes, adzes, arrow-heads, knives, and hoes. Of bone implements we have found awls, needles, and hair-pins. . . . The finds are similar to those of Yin-hsü, suggesting that these neolithic remains might represent the cultural elements of the pure Chinese stock ; the tools, for example, have certain peculiarities, which make them distinct from those found in Western China. . . . We hope, therefore, with these materials in hand, to make a thorough study which may not only throw light on the problem of early Shantung, but also increase our knowledge of the main problem before us, the origin of Chinese culture." (Translated from Bibl. 15, a leaflet consisting of one printed page.)

This excavation was not the final one. As it had produced many new problems which were of vital importance for our future research in prehistoric archæology, we decided to spend another season on this site. When we came back to Chi-nan, it was really a great pleasure to me when I found that I was appointed to study most of the finds and make a report on them. In three months and a half I succeeded in completing an interim account of the main features of this site, and the first draft of the final report was ready in August, 1931, four months later. After the discovery of Black Pottery at Hou Kang in Honan in the spring of 1931, it was considered absolutely necessary for us to settle the questions about Lung-shan by means of another excavation. This time, under the leadership of Mr. Liang Ssŭ-yung, the work extended from 9th to 30th October. Besides other achievements we arrived at definite answers to the questions about the wall, the kilns, and the relationship between the two cultures. The finds were again handed over to me, and I took the opportunity to study the materials and to revise the first report. The revised report was completed in March, 1932 ; it was edited by Dr. Li, Mr. Liang, and Mr. Tung Tso-pin, each of whom also wrote some of the articles. Mr. Kuo Pao-chün also contributed. It was not published until 1934, under the title *Ch'êng-tzŭ-yai*.

On 2nd February, 1931, I went to An-yang to take part in the excavation of Hsiao T'un. On a Sunday I went for a walk along the River Huan with Mr. Liang who was keenly interested in the problem of neolithic culture. We finally stopped at a hillock north of Kao-lou Chuang, about 700 yards south-east of Hsiao T'un. There we found potsherds, stone tools, and a very clearly exposed cultural stratum in the south bank of the river. This site had already been noticed by Dr. Li and Mr. Tung in 1928. This time, however, we found a sort of black pottery which was very similar to that of Lung-shan in Shantung. Owing to the badly weathered surface of the sherds we did not venture so far as to identify this pottery with that of Lung-shan.

Henceforth, Mr. Liang wished to devote himself to this site, and he arranged with the leaders of the party to be released from the work at Hsiao T'un in order to start a trial excavation at this hillock, which was locally known as Hou Kang. After five days' digging, it became clear that the artifacts there represented a culture which was more related to Lung-shan in Shantung than to the culture of the Shang-Yin dynasty. During this time I was digging at Ssŭ-p'an Mo, west of Hsiao T'un. After finishing my daily work I used to walk to the hillock to see what Mr. Liang had done. I also examined carefully his finds which had been collected and put in the camp at Huan-shang Ts'un. In the course of time, facts became so convincing that I could not but admit that this site was of the same culture as that of Lung-shan. On 31st April I joined Mr. Liang, and there we worked together for twelve days. This season we found only two layers in this site, the top layer containing the Shang-Yin remains, and the lower containing objects characteristic of Lung-shan. The evidence of stratification made it clear that the Black Pottery culture was earlier than the Shang-Yin as represented by the site of Hsiao T'un. In the winter of the same year, 1931, after the second excavation at Lung-shan, Mr. Liang returned to Hou Kang for the purpose of making another excavation. He succeeded in finding a section of the site where the stratification consisted of three layers of cultural remains ; the top layer contained remains of the Shang-Yin type, the middle contained objects of the Lung-shan type, and the lowest contained relics of the so-called Yang-shao culture. This discovery was of prime archæological value, because it manifested the sequence of these three cultures, the relationships between which had hitherto been shrouded in mystery and uncertainty.

In April of 1932 I came to An-yang again to join in the regular work of the season. On the evening of my arrival, Mr. Wang Hsiang, an assistant of the Academia Sinica, showed me his recent collections and told me the story of his new discoveries. He had found two Black

Pottery sites and one Red Pottery site, all on the north bank of the Huan River, and two of them not far from Hsiao T'un. The next day I went with Mr. Wang and two other friends to see the two sites near Hsiao T'un. After an hour's pleasant walk along the beautiful Huan River, we reached the nearest site, Hou-chia Chuang, which seemed to welcome us with its red sherds scattered here and there on the surface. When we examined the potsherds carefully, we found among the red sherds a lot of grey ware of a later epoch. In contrast with the site of Hsiao T'un this place had no raised area by which it might be distinguished from the surrounding country. We remained here for a while, then proceeded westward for about a quarter of a mile, where we arrived at a rampart, known as the T'ung-lo Chai. Here we found a layer of Black Pottery with a grey pottery layer above it. That night I got permission from the party to make a trial excavation at Hou-chia Chuang. Work started next morning. After eight days' digging, a profitable return was yielded. We found that it was a Red Pottery site covered by a Black Pottery layer with a grey pottery layer above that.

One month later I went to take part in the excavation at Hsin Ts'un, which is about 27 miles west of the district town of Hsün Hsien, and 30 miles south of the Hsiao T'un site. Black Pottery was found at Hsin Ts'un by Mr. Kuo Pao-chün during his excavation of the tombs of the Wei State. I was then appointed to continue the digging at Ta-lai Tien, about $1\frac{1}{2}$ miles south of Hsin Ts'un. The work was started by Mr. Wang Hsiang and Mr. Liu Yao, and they found both Black and Red pottery. I worked there for nine days, and I found that the stratification was just the same as that of Hou Kang near An-yang, i.e. it consisted of a deposit of three successive cultural layers containing Red, Black, and grey pottery.

In the winter of 1932, when I went to explore the southern part of Shantung, somewhere near the Station of Lin-ch'êng on the Tientsin Pukow Railway, I found a site covered with ashy soil containing pieces of Black Pottery, shells, and stone implements on the surface. In 1933 another site of the same nature was discovered, in the same district by the inhabitants of An-shang Ts'un, and it was excavated by the Academia Sinica.

I left China and came to England in July, 1933, and in the summer of 1934 I received a letter from Mr. Wang Hsiang telling me that in Jih-chao, Shantung, he and Mr. Ch'i Yen-p'ei had found a number of places where Black Pottery existed in plenty. So far only one site had been properly explored, namely the one near Liang-ch'êng. There he found two stone implements, fifteen black ware vessels more or less complete, and over a hundred fragments of the same ware. In the summer of 1935, when I went back to China on my archæological visit, I was able to see this collection. In 1936 this site was excavated by the Academia Sinica.

In the winter of 1934 Mr. Li Ching-tan and Mr. Wang Hsiang of the Academia Sinica found Black Pottery at Shou Hsien, Anhui (Bibl. 17, pp. 266–7), and in 1936 Mr. Li found a Black Pottery site at Tsan Hsien, a place situated at the tip of the narrow strip of Honan which lies between Kiangsu and Anhui. At the end of 1936 Mr. Shih Hsin-kung, of the West Lake Museum at Hang-chou, in Chêkiang discovered an ancient site where some black sherds were found in association with a few stone tools. In March, 1937, the discoverer, Mr. Shih, kindly sent me a detailed account of his discovery and three photographs of pots. So far as I can judge from the pictures and the information he gave me, I should say that the influence of Black Pottery had once reached as far as Hang-chou Bay, which is south of the Yang-tze River.

Thus within the last ten years, more than fifteen Black Pottery sites have been discovered and investigated.

Section 6.—Before closing the narrative of the prehistoric pottery discoveries, I must announce the aim of this thesis. The most fascinating problems of Chinese archæology, namely the origin of the Chinese culture, and the relationship between China and the West in ancient times have been revived, mainly owing to the discovery of the Red Pottery, the painted designs on which seem to some scholars to have affinities to those on Western wares. The discovery of the Black Pottery, representing another distinct early culture, has on the one hand thrown some light on the beginnings of the Shang-Yin culture, and on the other, it has raised another problem, that is the relationship between the Red Pottery and the Black Pottery cultures. Up to the present none of these problems has been solved. This thesis is intended to serve as the first step towards their solution. It is clear that the origins of any culture and the relationships between this culture and that cannot be discovered before the relative date of the finds is ascertained, and the relative date cannot be ascertained before completing a certain fundamental study. As far as prehistoric pottery is concerned, this study must include an analytical study of the pottery from the various prehistoric sites, a comparative study of the pottery characteristics of the various provincial groups, and a synthetic study of all the pottery types. The aim of this thesis is to accomplish this fundamental piece of work.

Section 7.—This thesis was written under the direction of Professor W. Perceval Yetts, University of London, to whose guidance and advice as well as encouragement I am indebted more deeply than I can say. Most of my technical knowledge I have acquired at the Central School of Arts and Crafts, London, under the supervision of Miss D. M. Billington. My thanks are due to Miss E. M. Hake, who has been kind enough to correct my English and also has given me valuable criticism.

Without the generous help of the officials of the National Research Institute of History and Philology, Academia Sinica, I should not have been able to collect so much valuable material. Among them Mr. Fu Ssŭ-nien, Dr. Li Chi, Mr. Tung Tso-pin, Mr. Liang Ssŭ-yung, and Mr. Kuo Pao-chün must be mentioned especially, for each helped me in many ways. To other friends of the same Institute— Mr. Liu Yü-hsia, Mr. Li Ching-tan, Mr. Shih Chang-ju, Mr. Liu Yao, Mr. Ch'i Yen-pei, Mr. Wang Hsiang, and Mr. Li Kuang-yü— my thanks are also due.

I wish to acknowledge my obligation to Dr. W. H. Wong,

Director of the Geological Survey of China, Professor P. L. Yüan of the Tsing Hua University, and Professor Hsü Ping-ch'ang and Mr. Ho Shih-chi of the National Research Institute of Pei-p'ing, for help of various kinds.

To the Government of Shantung I am indebted for the scholarship to study in England, and I have to thank the Universities' China Committee in London for a grant which enabled me to pay a short visit to China to collect information concerning newly excavated material.

The publication of this book has been aided with a grant from the Publication Fund of the University of London and gifts from Sir Percival David, Bt. and Mr. George Eumorfopoulos.

PART II

THE POTTERY GROUPS

CHAPTER I

THE NORTHERN HONAN GROUP

Section 8.—Under the Northern Honan group I shall describe the pottery finds from the following sites : Hou Kang, Hou-chia Chuang, Hsiao T'un, and other sites now being explored, viz. Ta-lai Tien, Hsin Ts'un, and Liu Chuang.

HOU KANG

My description is based on Mr. Liang's writings, Bibl. 19 and 20, and on my own observation.

Section 9.—The site of Hou Kang is about $1\frac{3}{4}$ miles north-west of the city of An-yang. It is so named, Hou Kang, or the Back Hillock, because its location is just behind, or north of, the village of Kao-lou Chuang. The River Huan flows on its northern side and the site of Hsiao T'un is only 263 yards north-west of it, while the P'ing-Han Railway is 273 yards east of it. The ground plan of the hillock is more or less elliptical, with an E.–W. diameter of 240 yards and a N.–S. diameter of 328 yards. The highest part of the hillock is not at the centre, but at a spot near the north side of the site. The slopes on the south, the west, and on the north-east are very gentle, but those on the east and the north are comparatively steep. The cultural areas cover the top part of the hillock to an extent of about 78,000 square yards.

The deposits on this site are of two kinds, (1) Shang-Yin layer above a Black Pottery layer, and (2) Black Pottery layer above a Red ware layer. As the contents of the Black Pottery layer in both kinds of deposits are the same, it may be stated with certainty that they occurred from first to last in the following sequence : red ware, black ware, and Shang-Yin ware.

Section 10.—The pottery finds from this site may be classified and described as follows :—

A. Plain,   B. Decorated.
  1. Red,
  2. Black,
  3. Grey.

A 1. Plain Red Ware.

(*a*) Colour.—The pottery finds from the bottom layer at Hou Kang are mainly plain red ware. This kind of ware and also the same ware with painted designs are well known as the " Yang-shao " ware, because the first discovery was made at Yang-shao Ts'un in Honan. But we are going to drop this name because it is unsuitable and misleading. Before we have grasped the relationship between the group under discussion and the so-called " Yang-shao " group from Western Honan, it would be rash to call them both by the same name. If we take only a few superficial resemblances as our criteria to identify their relationship we shall be forced to apply this name to all the early red wares found in the vast territory stretching from the Liao-tung Peninsula of Southern Manchuria to the Kokonor region of Ch'ing-hai. The distance between these points is no less than 2,000 miles, and within it are several different races and cultures which date from the beginnings of Chinese history. Therefore, in this thesis we shall not use the term " Yang-shao " except to denote the Yang-shao Ts'un site itself. The plain fine red ware and also the painted ware of the same technique we chose to call Red Pottery as their colour is generally red.

(*b*) Shape.—The shapes are extremely simple. Except a few fragments of water-jars, the bulk of the ware consists of bowls (Fig. V, *a*) varying in size.

(*c*) Material.—The quality of the clay is very fine. Sand is rarely visible to the naked eye.

(*d*) Thickness.—The average thickness is about 6 mm.

(*e*) Method of Making.—There is no trace of the potter's wheel.

The pots were made by hand with the help of a mould, or made by ring-building on the turn-table. I shall describe the moulding method in connection with Hou-chia Chuang (Section 13, pp. 28–30). The ring-building method was probably as follows : the clay was shaped into rolls or flat bands which were built up in coils until the desired size and shape of a vessel had been attained. A turn-table is simply a wooden disk pivoted on a stand.

(*f*) Surface Treatment.—A smooth surface was preferred. It was smoothed with a tool when the ware was still damp.

A 2. Plain Black Ware.

The black ware was commonly found in the middle layer. The plain fine grey ware of this same layer must be classed with plain black ware, because it corresponds in detail to the typical black ware. Sometimes the black ware was incised with simple designs.

This type of pottery is called the Lung-shan ware, because it was first discovered at the Ch'êng-tzŭ Yai site near Lung-shan village in Shantung. But unfortunately the term Lung-shan ware has been used to designate also the grey, white, and red pottery from that site. In this thesis we shall reserve the term " Lung-shan ware " for the black ware found at Ch'êng-tzŭ Yai, and the term " typical Lung-shan ware " for the thin shiny black ware found at any site other than Ch'êng-tzŭ Yai. Ordinary black wares found at any site will be called simply " Black Pottery ".

(*a*) Colour.—The typical black Lung-shan ware is very rare. The common type is black on the outside, but grey inside.

(*b*) Shape.—The forms and sizes are more varied than the Red Pottery ; the following shapes have been found though in a fragmentary state : bowls (Fig. I, *a*), deep bowls (Fig. I, *b*), tall jars (Fig. I, *c*), and basins (Fig. I, *d*).

(*c*) Material.—The clay used is still fine, but apparently coarser than that of the Red Pottery.

(*d*) Thickness.—The ware is thicker than the red ware, but the wall is still uniformly even. The average thickness is about 6 mm.

(*e*) Method of making.—This ware is wheel-made. The spiral, a typical feature of wheel technique, is sometimes clearly shown on the bases of the pots and the striæ are visible not only on the surface of the upper part of the vessel, but also all over the body.

(*f*) Surface treatment.—The surface was often burnished on the wheel, when the pot was nearly dry. This process was commonly used in making the black Lung-shan ware in Shantung.

A 3.   Plain Grey Ware.

All the pottery from the top layer may be grouped under this type, which is the product of the Shang-Yin period. I shall find it necessary to describe it in connection with Hsiao T'un (Section 16, pp. 36–39). There is, however, one kind of grey ware made of coarse and gritty material, which is found in the bottom layer. That is to say, it is the product of the Red Pottery period.

(*a*) Colour.—The colour is either grey or light brick-red.

(*b*) Shape.—The only shape is the *ting*, which is a cooking pot with three solid legs (Fig. IV, *a*). This *ting* is different from the *ting* of Yang-shao (Fig. LX). The differences are : the absence of basket-work imprints, and of small lugs ; the peculiar shape of the legs (Fig. IV, *b*, *c*, *d*, *e*, and *f*) ; and the rounded instead of the flat bottom.

(*c*) Material.—The material is coarse.

(*d*) Thickness.—The average thickness is about the same as that of the plain red ware.

(*e*) Method of making.—This ware is modelled by hand.

(*f*) Surface treatment.—The surface is smooth but not well polished.

There are two other kinds of plain grey ware, which are rare at this site, though they are definitely the products of the Black Pottery period, that means to say they are to be found in Hou Kang II. They are : (1) gritty ware, sometimes brown, with a typical imprint of squares on the surface (Fig. II, *a*), and (2) a ware of finer material, baked hard, with a typical imprint of broad matting band on the surface, though mostly smoothed down (Fig. II, *b* and *c*). The shapes

24

of this ware are jars and *li* (Fig. I, *e*), which is a cooking pot with three hollow legs.

B. Decorated Ware.

By " decorated " I mean both the painted ware and the incised ware. With the exception of the method of execution of the designs, the other technical details are more or less the same in these two wares.

(*a*) Colour.—Brick-red is the common colour of this ware. In the painted ware a darker red is applied to a lighter red surface. The firing of the incised ware is more accomplished than that of the painted ware, as is evident from the products which are burnt red throughout.

(*b*) Shape.—The common shapes are bowls. The mouth is mostly broad, and the base rounded (Fig. V).

(*c*) Material.—Judged by the surface, this ware sometimes appears to be more refined than the plain ware.

(*d*) Thickness.—The thickness is equal to that of the plain red ware.

(*e*) Method of making.—The method of making is the same as that of the plain red ware.

(*f*) Surface treatment.—The surface is either smoothed or polished.

(*g*) Decoration.—The designs are simple. Those of the painted ware may be classified into three groups : (1) broad band on the rim (Fig. V, *f*) ; (2) vertical lines along the rim (Fig. V, *a*) ; and (3) triangles filled in with parallel lines (Fig. V, *b*, *c*, *d*, *e*, and *f*). The designs on the incised ware are only of two kinds : (1) triangles filled in with parallel lines (Fig. III, *b*), the same as the third group of the painted designs ; and (2) triangular spaces filled in with criss-cross lines (Fig. III, *a*). These designs belong to the same type as is found on the imprinted wares (Fig. II, *a*).

Section 11.—The pottery from the top layer of this site is of the same type as that of Hsiao T'un II, which was inhabited by the Shang-Yin probably from the time of the nineteenth to the thirtieth sovereign. This period, according to the traditional chronology, was from about 1395–1122 B.C.

The Black Pottery from the middle layer is wheel-made like that of Lung-shan in Shantung. The highly burnished and very thin sherds are also like those of Lung-shan. On the whole, the black colour is not so pronounced as that of the Lung-shan ware.

The red ware from the bottom layer is of the same type and period as the red ware of Hou-chia Chuang. Its date must be earlier than the Yang-shao ware in Western Honan for the following reasons : the technique on the whole is more primitive than that of Yang-shao ; all the designs with the exception of two, and all the shapes are simpler than those of Yang-shao. The two sherds with complicated designs from this site, were neither of them found in the proper Red Pottery layer. One came from the top layer, Shang-Yin, and the other from the mixed layer between the top and the middle, or Black Pottery layer (Bibl. 20, p. 559).

HOU-CHIA CHUANG

In 1936 I published an article in Chinese on the pottery from this site, see Bibl. 32.

Section 12.—The Hou-chia Chuang site is situated on the north bank of the Huan River, about half a mile west of the village of Hou-chia Chuang and 4 miles north-west of An-yang. Its stratification is similar to that of Hou Kang ; Red Pottery in the bottom layer, Black Pottery in the middle layer, and grey pottery in the top layer. But the strata are not so clearly marked as those of Hou Kang. We found only a few places where three successive strata could be recognized.

Section 13.—The pottery from Hou-chia Chuang may be classified and described as follows :—

Plain Ware,	Decorated Ware,
A. Fine,	A. Painted Red,
1. Red,	B. Imprinted Black.
2. Black and Grey.	
B. Coarse Grey.	

Plain Ware A 1, Fine Red.

(*a*) Colour.—This ware is either brick-red throughout with the outer surface darker, or red on the outer surface and grey underneath. The colouring of the bowls shows certain peculiar features: there is a band of red round the rim while the rest of the bowl is grey both inside and out. That is the general rule. But there are two variations : entirely grey inside and red outside, or red inside with a red band like the others round the rim. The red band is generally sharply marked as if it had been made by mechanical means. How can we explain the occurrence of two colours on the outer surface ? If the upper or the lower part of the bowl had been covered with a layer of a different kind of material, we should expect to find signs of such a process. But it is quite obvious that the whole bowl was made of the same material and the surface had undergone a uniform treatment.

The red colour in wares of this period is produced by firing under oxidizing conditions and the grey colour by firing under reducing conditions. The red rim of the bowl is therefore due to the condition under which the pottery was fired. I believe that the red band was burnt in direct contact with air while the grey portion was protected from the air. But how could this be done in one and the same kiln ? I noticed that the diameter of the top line of the grey portion is more or less the same as the diameter of the mouth. I suggest that these bowls were burnt in piles, one on top of the other ; perhaps more than ten in one pile. This was necessary in order to save space in the kiln. The lower part of one bowl being covered by the bowl in which it rested, must have been burnt under reducing conditions and thus became grey. By this method only the top and bottom bowls in the pile would be different from the others. The inside of the top bowl and the outside of the bottom bowl would be exposed to the air and so became red.

There are a few sherds of pure grey colour but they are of the same technique as the red ware. Judging by their shape, most of them might have been fragments of bowls, such as those described.

27

(*b*) Shape.—As the pottery finds from this site are in a very fragmentary state it is very difficult to judge exactly how many shapes there are in this class. At least we may be quite sure of the following shapes :

1. Small bowls. (Fig. VI, 1–7, and Fig. VII, *a*).
2. Large bowls. (Fig. VI, 8–12).
3. Jars of various sizes (Fig. VI, 13–17), jars with a flat base (Fig. VI, 20–2).
4. Water bottles with a narrow mouth and neck, a broad belly, and a flat base (Fig. VI, 18–19). These bottles are different from the water containers of Western Honan, in that they have a flat instead of a pointed base.
5. Tripods or *ting*, three-footed vessels with solid legs.

(*c*) Material.—The material of this ware appears to be well prepared, as the clay is always fine and uniform. The ancient potters must have learned through long experience that the clay should be properly prepared in order to avoid cracking and distortion in the course of drying and firing.

The material of this type of ware may be divided into three kinds : (1) Very fine clay, sometimes mixed with very fine sand. (2) Fine clay which is either washed clay or river silt. (3) Clay mixed with sand.

(*d*) Thickness.—The thickness, especially that of the bowl, is uniformly even. The thickness is 2–7 mm. for bowls, and 3–9 mm. for deep and large vessels.

(*e*) Method of making.—From a study of the signs on the sherds, I have come to the conclusion that there were two methods of making pottery in this period. For larger vessels the ring-building method was used, and the process of building was always done on a turn-table. When the vessel was nearly finished, the potter used one hand to spin the turn-table as quickly as possible, while with the other he gripped the rim, so as to give it a well-defined edge. That is why we can always find fine lines, or striæ, running parallel with the rim like those made by wheel-technique. The depth of the striæ is about 3 inches, corresponding to the length of a finger.

28

For smaller vessels, such as bowls, the moulding method was used. But this method was quite different from the moulding methods of the Shang-Yin and Chou. We will take this opportunity to explain it in detail.

The shape of the mould must be hemispherical and its surface smooth. It was perhaps made of clay, or wood, or it might have been one half of a gourd. The turn-table was also used for the special purpose of finishing the rim.

The clay was applied on to the inner side of the mould and then pressed even. The custom is to put on more clay than is really required, and then to scoop out the surplus with a tool in order to get the proper thickness. After scooping, the surface was smoothed with the wet hand, or in the case of water containers for which no smooth inner surface is necessary, the scooping marks were left, and they are clearly visible. The outer surface is always smooth and even, presenting an appearance much like that resulting from the wheel-technique. Sometimes in making the *ting* and other cooking vessels, the mould was used in a different way. Instead of applying the clay on to the inside of the mould it was put on outside. That is why the inner surface of such vessels is always smooth and the outer surface shows signs of having been tooled.

The processes of moulding may be surmised by careful scrutiny of the signs on the surface of the vessels. So far as I can see, the making of small bowls was different from the making of larger vessels. For small bowls clay was laid round the inner surface of the mould in a series of rings having the form of cylinders or flattened bands, or it might be applied in small lumps. The clay was pressed with a pottery pestle, so as to make the wall even and the inner surface smooth. Bowls made by this method always have very smooth surfaces, both outside and inside. The ware is rendered very compact by the pressure of the pestle. In making larger vessels, the pestle was seldom used, though the mould was still required. The clay was applied on to the mould in the same way as in the process of making bowls, but the surface was simply smoothed down with the wet hand.

29

Having these processes in mind we shall now be able to understand why this type of red ware has the following characteristics : (1) The shape tends to be hemispherical (Fig. VII, *a*), because the mould itself was hemispherical. (2) The section of the wall tends to be thinner toward the bottom and thicker toward the rim (Fig. VI, 6–9), because more pressure is exerted on the bottom of the mould than on the other parts. (3) Some of the rims are flattened (Fig. VI, 6) as if they had been made by cutting away the clay from the edge of the mould. (4) As regards surfaces there are certain differences to be noted : except the cooking pots, the outer surface of all these vessels is always smooth and even. Except the bowls, the inner surface is quite different from the outer surface. The presence of scooping marks, clear and deep impressions of the hand and signs of tooling are quite common. (5) The curve of the moulded surface is regular (Fig. VI, 1–9).

(*f*) Surface treatment.—In contrast with the surface of the Black Pottery the surface of this ware is not so well finished. But it is always smooth and of a very delicate texture. Except the bowls, the inner surface is, as a rule, not so well finished as the outer. The methods used to improve the surface, so far as we can tell, are as follows :—

(1) Smoothing with the wet hand during the process of making.
(2) Smoothing with a tool when the vessel was still damp.
(3) Polishing with an object, such as a pebble. This had to be done when the vessel was nearly dry.

Some pots have parallel horizontal grooves about 3 mm. wide all over the surface.

Plain Ware A2, Black and Grey.

(*a*) Colour.—At this site we found no typical Lung-shan ware. The black colour varies from dark black to nearly grey. On a single vessel some parts are black and some either dark or light grey. A few vessels are entirely grey, though they have all the other characteristics of the proper black ware. As we can see from the fracture, the black ware is only black on the surface and not black throughout. Through

30

the difference of colour in the fracture, we may divide the black ware into the following categories : black with grey core, black with purple core, black with red core, and black with red underneath and grey as the innermost core.

The variations of colour may be seen most clearly in the more or less complete vessels. Some vessels are black both on the outer and inner surface, but the shiny lustre seldom occurs on the inner surface as it does on the outer surface. Some vessels are black on the outer surface but grey or in a few cases red on the inner surface.

(b) Shape.—Judging by the shapes of the rims (Fig. VI, 23–9), and the few complete pots which remain (Fig. VII, b and c), the forms of the black ware are much more varied than those of the red ware.

(c) Material.—Except a very small proportion, which is just as fine as the red ware, the clay of the main bulk of black ware appears to be coarser than that of the red ware. Sand is quite often found in the body, but in varying proportions, sometimes the ware is nearly as coarse as that of cooking vessels of the Shang-Yin and Chou periods. The grains of sand also vary much in size.

The neglect of the proper preparation of the clay does not imply degeneration in the art of pottery-making. For example, the methods of drying the newly made wares and regulating the temperature of the kiln must have been improved, as there were no cracks or distortion produced although an inferior kind of clay was used. Long experience is shown in controlling the clay ; although the clay was inferior, the finished wares were much better in almost every respect than those of the Red Pottery period.

(d) Thickness.—The thickness varies from 4–12 mm., a greater range of variation than that shown by the Red Pottery. The body appears to be less compact in texture than the red ware. This is not only because its material is coarser and thickness greater, but also because it was made in a slightly different way. In making red ware the clay was pressed hard against the inside of the mould, and this had the effect of producing a compact ware. In making Black Pottery much less pressure was used, as I shall explain.

31

(*e*) Method of making.—The manufacture of the black ware is obviously more advanced than that of the red ware ; the processes were more complicated. Judging from the signs on the sherds we may identify three methods of manufacture as follows :—

(1) In making small vessels, the ring-building method of the Red Pottery period was still practised and the use of the turn-table was more common than in the former period. In making larger vessels, the ring-building was done upon the turn-table with the help of a mould, which differed from the hemispherical mould of the former period : it was a curved strip or belt presumably of wood, bamboo, or pottery about 2 inches wide and 10 inches long. I shall subsequently refer to this as a " belt-mould ". The first strip of clay was laid on the mould, and smoothed down with the hand ; the belt-mould was then pulled away and used again to continue the wall until the required height was reached. But the part near the rim of the vessel was usually made by the ordinary ring-building method.

(2) In making small shallow vessels, such as dishes and bowls, the turn-table was sometimes used in this way : one hand turned the table, while the other held the clay and shaped it to the required form.

(3) Large deep vessels, especially those for cooking purposes, were made by another method. The belt-mould was still used but the strip of wood, or pottery, was bound round with string or cord, from one end to the other. The mould was always used in a horizontal position, and consequently the imprints of the string run in vertical lines (Figs. VIII and IX). There are two indications of such a mould having been used : the imprints on the outer surface of the vessel and the remains of hand pressure on the inner surface. Wherever the hand pressed with greater force on the inner surface the imprints on the outer surface appeared sharper. Sometimes these two indications have been almost obliterated. Only through careful scrutiny can one find some traces of them. The purpose of binding the mould with string or cord was clearly not to produce a decorative pattern, as we find quite often that efforts were made to destroy the impressions of string left on the pot. On large vessels

32

such partly obliterated impressions have left visible traces. Therefore, this binding of string or cord must have served a practical purpose. I made some experiments in moulding, and I found by experience that the clay was liable to stick to the mould, especially when the clay was fine and the mould wet. In order to prevent the clay sticking I was forced to bind the mould with string.

This belt-mould may be regarded as the forerunner of the later " beater and pad " method, in which a pad is put inside the vessel while the outside is beaten with a beater made of straw matting, or pottery impressed with matting designs. Likewise we may say that the hemi-spherical mould of the Red Pottery period was the ancestor of the belt-mould. This is certainly an improvement : there is no need to wait for the clay to dry before removing it from the mould ; and various shapes and sizes can be produced. Three peculiar features were produced by this method. The wall is less uniform than in the red ware, and the vessels are always flat-bottomed, because they were built up on a turn-table. Signs of pressure or smoothing by hand are clearly seen on the inside surface.

(f) Surface treatment.—A smooth surface was still preferred in this period. String impressions were sometimes smoothed down in order to get the desired effect. Polishing was sometimes done with a smooth round object when the vessel was nearly dry. Sometimes the vessel was simply smoothed by hand, or with a tool. The shiny surface was produced by burnishing on the turn-table when the vessel was nearly dry.

Plain Ware B, Coarse Grey.

This ware is definitely not prehistoric. But for the sake of comparison and in order to show the stages of the development of the grey pottery, we shall describe its main features.

(a) Colour.—The colour is mainly grey, varying from almost black to light grey. The colours of the fracture are the following : grey outside, red inside ; red throughout, or practically so (this is rare) ; dark grey or nearly black on the outside with red inside.

(b) Shape.—The shapes are much more complicated and the

sizes more varied than those of the Black Pottery. The common shape is the tall jar (Fig. VI, 30–2, and Fig. VII, *e*) ; more than 400 fragments of this type of jar were found during the excavation.

(*c*) Material.—The material is coarse. Sand is mixed with clay in a constant proportion. The proportion of sand is greater in cooking vessels than in any other pots.

(*d*) Thickness.—The sherds are rough on the surface but uniform, with an average thickness of about 6 mm.

(*e*) Method of making.—In this type of ware we can find not only the well-developed technique of the earlier periods but some new methods as well : (1) Ring-building on a turn-table with the help of a belt-mould. This is a method known in the Black Pottery period, but the following are new. (2) Hand-made ware with beaten or impressed string-impressions. (3) Wheel-made ware with string-impressions beaten or impressed on the surface. (4) Wheel-made ware.

(*f*) Surface treatment.—Nearly the whole outer surface was covered with string-impressions, and only the rim left plain. The base and sometimes the lower part of the vessel may show signs of having been scratched with a tool. The inner surface of the wheel-made ware is always fairly smooth, though the outer surface may be rough. But the hand-made wares always show signs of pressing and smoothing by hand on the inner surface.

In my opinion, in this period the string-impressions were in most cases produced in a new way. A wooden rolling-pin bound round with string, or a piece of rope, about the length of one's palm, i.e. 4 inches, was rolled over the surface of a newly made and still wet vessel so that the marks of the string or rope were left on it. This shows that the belt-mould was no longer favoured, and the wheel had become popular. The potters made these impressions deliberately in order to reproduce the characteristics of former times. It was simply an act of conservatism, just as the artisans of the Black Pottery period often purposely obliterated the string impressions caused by the mould, because they were trying to imitate the smooth surface favoured in former times.

Decorated Ware A, Painted Red.

The painted ware forms an extremely small proportion of the red ware from this site. The colour, material, thickness, and method of making are all identical with those of the ordinary red ware. The only peculiarity is that no other shape has been found except bowls.

The designs were painted either in dark red or purplish black. This difference in colour is due to the conditions of firing and not to the use of different pigments. The designs are very simple as can be seen in Figs. X–XV, but there is the possibility, as revealed by Fig. XIV, that some more complicated designs, though not necessarily so complicated as those of the Western Honan group, may be found if more extensive excavation of this site is made.

Decorated Ware B, Imprinted Black.

There are among the black ware a few pieces bearing imprinted designs as shown in Fig. XVI. These ornaments were made by impressing a die on to the surface when the vessel was still moist. The other techniques of this ware are the same as those of the black ware.

Section 14.—The grey pottery of this site belongs to a historic period. Judging by the similarity of its pottery forms (Fig. VII, *d, e*) to those found at Lung-shan II in Shantung, we are safe in saying that this type of ware at Hou-Chia Chuang may be dated to the time of Eastern Chou. There is a gap of hundreds of years between the Black and the grey pottery layers.

The Black Pottery of this site is more primitive in technique than that of either Hou Kang or Lung-shan. Not a single piece of the typical Lung-shan ware has been found there. So far as I am aware, this is the earliest type of Black Pottery discovered in China up to the present.

The red ware, which is the same as that of Hou Kang, is so much more primitive in technique as compared with the Western Honan group that I am strongly inclined to date it very early in the history of painted pottery.

35

Hsiao T'un

Section 15.—The Hsiao T'un site is named after the village about 2 miles north-west of the district town of An-yang Hsien in Honan. The ancient remains are found right underneath this village and the fields north of it within the sharp bend of the Huan River. Since 1899 the value of the finds from this site has been recognized. It was only in 1928, however, that the Academia Sinica started the systematic excavation which is still going on at the present day.

The Hsiao T'un deposit consists of two layers ; the upper one belongs to the Shang-Yin, and the lower to the Black Pottery period (Bibl. 25, p. 724). Pottery forms the main bulk of the finds, while artifacts of stone, bone, shell, horn, and bronze are also found. The pottery finds are very fragmentary : only very few complete pots have been recovered, chiefly from tombs.

Pottery finds from the Shang-Yin layer are really beyond our scope, but I have described them, because I find such a description necessary in order to complete the chronological sequence in the Third Part of this thesis.

Section 16.—The pottery finds from this site may be classified and described as follows :—

A. Plain,
  1. Coarse,
    (a) Grey,
    (b) Red.
  2. Fine,
    (a) Black,
    (b) Grey.

B. Decorated,
  1. Incised,
  2. Painted.

C. White Ware.

A 1a. Plain Coarse Grey Ware.

(a) Colour.—The colour is grey of a uniform tone throughout. Judging by modern parallels, I believe that this uniformity of colour was produced by the " yin-yao " or imbibing method. After the baking process was complete and the fire had died down, the top of the kiln was covered with alternate layers of wet straw and earth, on which water was poured in small quantities at a time. In this way the atmosphere of the kiln gradually became impregnated with moisture.

(*b*) Shape.—The shapes, so far as can be ascertained by the large sherds, are more than fifty, including bowls, basins, and jars. Many vessels are very large in size, much larger than the vessels of the previous periods. The round bottom (Fig. XVII) is a common feature and the ring-foot is sometimes attached to the round base to make the vessel stable. Some vessels show close similarity to bronze shapes ; the *li* of Fig. XVIII is a good example.

(*c*) Material.—The clay, especially that of the cooking vessels, is mixed with sand.

(*d*) Thickness.—Few sherds are less than about 15 mm. thick. The wall of ordinary vessels is as thick as about 20–30 mm. The thick walls of the ware at this site are in contrast to the thinner walls of the red, and black wares of the earlier periods, which precede the Shang-Yin. The wall is neither as uniform, nor as even, as that of the hand-modelled or wheel-made ware.

There are also a few specimens of thin-walled gritty ware with vertical string-impressions which belong to the first period of Hsiao T'un.

(*e*) Method of making.—This ware A 1*a* is mainly made by the beater and pad method, which for the sake of brevity I sometimes call the " beater method " in this thesis. Ring-building is used to a much smaller extent.

The beater method is still practised in making large water-jars in Northern China to-day. This is the process : after the form of a vessel is roughly fashioned its wall is beaten into the desired thickness with an instrument, known as the beater. In beating it is necessary to press a pad on the inner surface, therefore the inner surface shows distinct, but shallow pits left by the pad. These pits are never found on the base or the rims, because those parts are not made by beating. The beater, which is made of a thin rectangular strip of wood, is bound round with string ; the surface of the pad is coated with some soft stuff such

37

as leather, or cloth. I believe that in ancient times the beater and pad were not much different from these.

(*f*) Surface treatment.—The string-impressions of the beater are different from those of the belt-mould. Both appear on the outer surface, but the impressions of the beater are shallow and appear in small groups each of which covers a certain fixed area (Fig. XVII), while the impressions made by the belt-mould are deep and distinct and always run in the same direction. As regards the inner surface, the marks of the pad are often clear on the beaten ware, and on the moulded ware there are no such marks, but only the marks of smoothing with the hand.

The various kinds of string-impressions were sometimes destroyed in the process of trimming, especially those on the base and on the shoulder, which was sometimes decorated with incised designs after the surface was smoothed in this way.

The wares made by ring-building may also have string-impressions. So far as I can see, they were imprinted by means of an instrument which may be called a roller. It is simply a short round rod covered with a continuous line of string. From the marks on the pots, I found that the length of the roller is about 45 mm. From the lower part of a round-bottomed jar I found that the string-impressions were rolled on first in a vertical and then in a horizontal direction. The inner surface of this kind of ware is always smooth.

A 1*b*. Plain Coarse Red Ware.

(*a*) Colour.—The colour is brick-red on the surface and grey in the core. The red colour must have been baked under conditions different from those under which the grey ware was baked.

(*b*) Shape.—There are two common shapes : the water-jar with round base, and the so-called " helmet " (Fig. XIX).

(*c*) Material.—Except the thin-walled cover (which the workmen call small helmet), the other pots of this ware are made of coarse gritty clay. The cover is made of the same kind of clay as the ordinary grey ware. The so-called " helmet " is made of gritty ware. It has been

38

regarded as a crucible for casting bronze (Bibl. 22, p. 684). But it bears no soot on any part of the outer surface, and it has no pouring lip. Its shape is unsuitable and its weight is far too heavy to be the cover of a vessel. I think it has a special function of its own. I noticed in the fracture of the wall of its belly the clear dividing marks of four or five layers. It seemed to me that the capacity of the vessel had been tested and corrected several times before it was baked. So I venture to suggest that the helmet is really a Shang-Yin measure.

(*d*) Thickness.—The red sherds are usually thinner than the grey ones, and the average thickness is about 10 mm. But the helmet must be regarded as an exception. Its thickest part is more than 25 mm.

(*e*) Method of making.—This ware is moulded. The helmet is made by two kinds of moulds ; the base is made by a belt-mould and the body is made with the aid of a mould covered with a textile fabric. That is why we find that the lower part, near the base, has string-impressions and the upper part square-shaped impressions of textiles, while the inside surface has marks of having been smoothed with the wet hand. The rim is trimmed and finished on a turn-table, and therefore parallel striæ are often left upon it. Judging by the marks left on the base of the helmet, the size of the mould is about 70 by 30 mm.

(*f*) Surface treatment.—The surface was untouched, because the rough surface suited the purpose for which these wares were made.

A 2*a*. Fine Black Ware.

(*a*) Colour.—The colour of this type of ware is generally black. On the whole, the black colour of the Hsiao T'un ware is lighter than that of the typical Lung-shan ware. Dark grey is quite common.

(*b*) Shape.—Basins, bowls, and jars are the common shapes.

(*c*) Material.—The clay is fine and was well prepared by some refining process.

(*d*) Thickness.—The black sherds are sometimes as thin as typical Lung-shan ware, and the appearance is very similar to it. The average thickness is about 1·5 mm.

(*e*) Method of making.—By its make, the black ware from Hsiao

T'un may be divided into three categories : the moulded ware of Hou-chia Chuang type, the wheel-made ware of Hou Kang type, and the ware made by beating or moulding which is peculiar to this site. The impressions of the mould were smoothed down, though sometimes traces of them are still visible, but the inner surface is typical of the moulded ware. The black ware made by the beater method often has marks of the pad on the inner surface, but the outer surface can hardly be differentiated from the moulded ware.

On the lids of some black wares I have noticed striæ made by the wheel on the outer surface, and the marks of the pad on the inner surface. So we see that the vessel was originally made by means of the beater method and finally finished on the wheel.

The black wares are, as a rule, small in size. All the large vessels of the Shang-Yin period are not made of black, but of grey ware.

(*f*) Surface treatment.—Burnishing on the wheel is the common method. The surface of the moulded, or beaten, ware is polished, and the marks of polishing are often very distinct. A polished surface is smooth and glossy, but it has no signs of any parallel lines like those produced by burnishing. Hand or tool-marks are clear on the inner surface and these are typical of the moulded ware.

A 2*b*. Plain Fine Grey Ware.

(*a*) Colour.—The grey is of a light tone, like the so-called silver grey.

(*b*) Shape.—Cups, bottles, and jars are sometimes found. The prototype of the *tou*, known as *min*, is common. A *min* (Fig. XXXIV, 12) is different from the *tou* (Fig. XXXIV, 13), or stemmed cup, for its stem is much shorter and thicker than that of the *tou* (Bibl. 16, pp. 476–8).

(*c*) Material.—The clay is nearly as fine as that of the black ware.

(*d*) Thickness.—This ware is much thicker than the black ware, but thinner than the coarse grey ware.

(*e*) Method of making.—Only a few specimens of this ware are hand-modelled, but most of them are made by beating. I have noticed a number of sherds which have a polished shiny surface with signs of the pad on the inner surface. On the outer surface there are horizontal and parallel sunk or raised lines, showing that the pot, though made by beating, was finished on the wheel or the turn-table. There are no such lines on the inner surface, because it was not thus trimmed.

The *min* of Hsiao T'un may be mistaken for wheel-made wares, and only by careful observation is it possible to find out that they are beaten. On the outer surface of the base in the area inside the ring-foot, there are traces of string-impressions.

(*f*) Surface treatment.—The smoothing of the surface was often done on a turn-table, or perhaps a wheel. Some striæ parallel to the rim may appear, but the surface is quite different from the burnished surface of the black ware. It is smooth and delicate but not shiny.

B. Decorated Wares : 1, Incised ; 2, Painted.

(1) The incised ware is the same in technique as the plain coarse grey wares. The incised zigzag motifs are simple but typical of the Shang-Yin period.

(2) During the season of 1929, one piece of painted sherd was found in an undisturbed layer of inscribed bones and shells (Bibl. 14, p. 337). The curvature of the sherd suggests that it has been broken off from a bowl. The colour is brick-red, and its upper part is covered with a white slip. The painted designs are applied on to the slip in two colours, black and red (Fig. XX).

C. White Ware. (Plain and Decorated.)

(*a*) Colour.—The colour is white like the paste of modern stone ware, but the body is soft. The temperature at which the white ware was fired is estimated to be about 900–1,000° C. (Bibl. 28, Japanese text, p. 42), much lower than that of porcelain and stone wares.

(*b*) Shape.—The common shapes are *min*, while shapes similar to dishes and jars are rare.

(*c*) Material.—The material is china clay or kaolin (Bibl. 28,

Japanese text, p. 42). The softness of the ware is due to the rather low temperature at which it has been baked.

(d) Thickness.—The engraved white ware is always thick, but the plain white ware is fairly thin. The average thickness is about 6–10 mm.

(e) Method of making.—This ware was also made by the beater method. A few small sized vessels were modelled by hand.

(f) Surface treatment.—The impressions of the beater were generally destroyed, and the surface was smoothed with the wet hand.

(g) Decoration.—Sometimes the white ware pots were engraved with beautiful motifs of the same kind as those which appear on bronze vessels of the Shang-Yin period.

Section 17.—The excavation of Hsiao T'un has served as a guide to archæologists as far as the sequence of cultures is concerned. Hsiao T'un pottery represents nearly all the primitive techniques of the prehistoric sites, besides its own peculiarity, the employment of the beater and pad. In the Shang-Yin period particularly large vessels were in demand, and they could not be produced by means of the belt-mould. The wheel had not yet been thoroughly mastered. Therefore, the method of beater and pad was adopted. This method is merely an improved type of the moulding method ; the mould in the form of a beater became smaller and more movable.

Hsiao T'un was not inhabited in the Red Pottery period, but only later in the Black Pottery period, after which there was an interval of perhaps not more than a few centuries before the Shang-Yin people came with their typical coarse grey ware. After the downfall of the Shang-Yin, the Chou conquerors occupied a part of the site for a very short period, and soon it was abandoned altogether, and finally changed into farming fields and cemeteries.

The date of the Shang-Yin layer (Hsiao T'un II) is ascertained by the inscriptions and it agrees more or less with the traditional date, i.e. from P'an-kêng to Chou-hsin (c. 1395–1122 B.C.), while the date of the layer below it (Hsiao T'un I) must be the same as Hou Kang II as far as can be judged from pottery remains.

OTHER NORTHERN HONAN SITES NOW BEING EXPLORED

Section 18.—Ta-lai Tien.—The Ta-lai Tien site is situated about $1\frac{1}{2}$ miles south of the Hsün Hsien station on the P'ing-Han Railway ; its shape is, more or less, a square raised platform, the area of which is about 400 by 300 yards. This site was excavated in 1932 by the Academia Sinica and it was found to have a deposit of three layers : the first layer belongs to the Red Pottery period, the second to the Black Pottery period, the third to a grey pottery period. In other words, its stratification is like that of Hou-chia Chuang in Northern Honan.

The Red Pottery in the first layer is simple in shape (Fig. XXI–XXII) and design (Fig. XXIII) ; the rim is sometimes painted simply with a broad band in dark red. The black and grey wares are found together in the second layer and black ware is comparatively rare. In the third layer only the grey ware is found. A few specimens of black sherds are nearly as thin as the typical Lung-shan ware.

The pottery finds of the first layer are on the whole similar to those of Hou-chia Chuang I and the pottery in the second layer seems to represent a culture later than Hou Kang II, or the same as Hsin Ts'un in the same district. The pottery of the third layer is contemporary with Hou-chia Chuang III.

Section 19.—Hsin Ts'un.—The Hsin Ts'un site is situated about 2 miles west of the Hsün Hsien station on the P'ing-Han Railway, right on the north bank of the Ch'i River ; part of it is covered by the village Hsin Ts'un.

In the soil covered by the dwelling site, a cemetery of the early Chou period was made ; more than eighty tombs have been dug by the Academia Sinica since 1932.

Grey pottery sherds form the main bulk of the finds, black ware of the same type as that of Ta-lai Tien is found in a smaller proportion. The shapes of grey or black wares are numerous ; the cooking pot with three hollow legs, the *ting*, beaker, dish, bowl, basin, *min*, and jar are all found. The *li* is high and slender and of the Pu-chao Chai type. At this site the earliest type of beaten ware is found, the surface of which shows clear and typical marks of impressed squares. This beaten ware looks different from the moulded ware, and the following characteristics may be observed : because this ware was made by the beating method, the inner surface bears signs of the pad, but rarely that of the hand ; the impressions on the outer surface, which are in relief, consist of a series of identical marks. That shows that they are the products of the one and the same beater. This ware is a peculiar feature of Honan, not only Northern, but also Western ; for instance, it is found at Pu-chao Chai (Fig. LXI). But it has not been found among the Red Pottery, or among the later grey pottery. So it serves as a good criterion for identifying the Black Pottery culture.

As the tomb-diggers of the early Chou period had broken into the cultural remains of the dwelling site, it is obvious that the Hsin Ts'un site ceased to be a dwelling place before the beginning of the Chou. On the evidence of its pottery I suggest dating it later than Hou Kang II and about the same period as Ta-lai Tien II.

Section 20.—Liu Chuang.—The Liu Chuang site is situated south of the village by the same name, about 1 mile west of the Hsün Hsien station. The site itself is slightly higher than the surrounding ground. It was excavated by the Academia Sinica in 1933 and the finds are mainly Red Pottery.

The pottery is brick-red in colour of a very uniform tone, often the same throughout. The painted designs are characteristic of Northern Honan : parallel wavy lines in groups make the common design ; no white slip or polychrome is found, and the only colour is dark red.

The motifs are more complicated than those of other sites in Northern Honan. A peculiar motif is the double-hook turning upward, not unlike that of Hsin Tien in Kansu. I do not, however, feel justified in assuming on the evidence of this one similarity that these sites are contemporary.

The pottery of this site is more advanced than that of the other Northern Honan sites, but still not so highly developed as that of

44

Yang-shao in Western Honan. I think it is an advanced stage of the culture represented by Ta-lai Tien I.

Section 21.—Summing up the results of the study of the Northern Honan group, I have arranged the various sites in the following chronological order :—

(1) Hou Kang I, Hou-chia Chuang I, and Ta-lai Tien I.
(2) Liu Chuang.
(3) Hou-chia Chuang II.
(4) Hou Kang II and Hsiao T'un I.
(5) Hsin Ts'un and Ta-lai Tien II.
(6) Hou Kang III and Hsiao T'un II.
(7) Hou-chia Chuang III and Ta-lai Tien III.

CHAPTER II

THE WESTERN HONAN GROUP

Section 22.—The Western Honan group includes the pottery finds from seven sites : Yang-shao, Ch'in-wang Chai, Ch'ih-kou Chai, Pu-chao Chai, Ch'ên-Kou, Ch'ing T'ai, and T'a P'o.

YANG-SHAO TS'UN

Section 23.—The Yang-shao Ts'un site is situated 5 miles north of Mien-ch'ih Hsien on the southern slope of a range of hills in Western Honan. The pottery from this site is in a very fragmentary state, and intact specimens are extremely rare. Such conditions always obtain when a long-inhabited site is gradually abandoned. The first description of these ceramic finds is to be found in Dr. Andersson's article, *An Early Chinese Culture*, 1923 (Bibl. 1), but the first scholar who made a systematic study of this pottery is Dr. T. J. Arne, who, in his *Painted Stone Age Pottery from the Province of Honan, China, 1925* (Bibl. 6), dealt with more than 1,000 specimens from this site.

Section 24.—The pottery finds from Yang-shao may be classified and described as follows :—

A. Plain Ware,   B. Decorated Ware.

A. Plain Ware.

(*a*) Colour.—The colour of this type of ware is mainly grey, and sometimes red or brown. A few specimens of white ware are also found.

(*b*) Shape.—The shapes of this ware are mainly bowls, basins, water-jugs (Figs. XXIV, XXV) and *ting* (Fig. LX). The *ting* is very similar to Bronze Age shapes.

(*c*) Material.—The clay of this ware is not of such uniform quality

46

as that of the decorated ware. Generally speaking the clay is coarser than that of the decorated ware.

(d) Thickness.—The body is, on the whole, thicker and less even than that of the decorated ware.

(e) Method of making.—When he wrote the article *An Early Chinese Culture*, Dr. Andersson seems to have been puzzled about the method of making of this type of ware. He examined four pieces and found evidences both of hand and wheel technique. He describes a bowl, which is marked inside the rim with concentric regular lines suggesting wheel-technique, but the other parts of which seem to be hand-modelled (Bibl. 1, p. 49). He describes another bowl, on the outside of which, near the margin, numerous regular concentric lines seem to indicate wheel-technique, but the irregular bottom and the rest of the outer surface point to hand-work (ibid., p. 49). In describing a tumbler he says that the base and the outside surface indicate wheel-technique, but the inside surface is rough and irregular (ibid., p. 50). In a pot he notices that the outer surface is covered with nearly obliterated oblique basket patterns upon which are superimposed three sharp horizontal ridges. The whole vessel, including these ridges, is irregular in shape and apparently hand-made, but some kind of wheel-technique seems to have been used for shaping the rim, the edge of which is covered with fine regular striæ (ibid., p. 62).

Dr. Andersson believed, therefore, that he had found the evidence of wheel-technique, not only in these four specimens, but in others from Yang-shao. But I have noticed that these parallel striæ or regular lines always appear on the rim of a vessel but never on the base, or even the lower part. It may be suggested that the striæ on the body could have been obliterated by polishing or by constant use. But if that were so, we should expect to find striæ on the inner surface of the vessel undestroyed. The fact remains that only the rim, or the top part of the vessel, was made with the aid of some mechanism. In my opinion, this mechanism is the turn-table, not the wheel.

The coarse plain wares with mat-impressions are thought by Dr. Andersson to be hand-modelled. As regards those impressions on

47

the surface he gives a simple explanation : " the hand-made vessels are often formed upon a bed of cloth, matting, or basket work, the impressions of which are still distinctly visible as a constructional pattern, though this has in many cases been obliterated and replaced by later decorative patterns " (ibid., p. 28). This ingenious theory sounds very plausible, but it raises a new question. Why was such a bed of matting or basket-work necessary ? If such a bed had been used, on which to model the pot, the impressions must appear on the pot in overlapping irregular angles, as it had to be turned round and about in the process of making. But the impressions are actually as regular as if some mat or piece of basket-work had been applied once, and not interfered with again. So far as I can see, they are the impressions of the belt-mould such as was used in Northern Honan.

(f) Surface treatment.—The commonest type of surface of this ware is that with impressions of what Dr. Andersson supposes to be cord, mat, and basket-work. Those impressions should not be taken as ornaments, and they were never regarded as such because they were sometimes obliterated so as to give place to decorative patterns. It is my opinion that they were merely the marks of the mould in which the vessel was made. Sometimes the surface was smoothed with some sort of spatula while the ware was still damp, and this process could obliterate nearly all the mat-impressions. A few specimens were burnished and blackened to a shiny appearance like black leather.

B. Decorated Ware.

(a) Colour.—Usually the ware is burnt to a brick-red colour throughout. Some of the thick sherds are not so well burnt, and there is a grey core underneath the red surface. An interesting fact connected with the method of firing is shown by one of the bowls, which has a red margin round the rim and a grey body. Close to the rim the fracture is red throughout ; lower down we find a grey core which becomes thicker and thicker until the body is grey throughout. Dr. Andersson explains this state as due to insufficient oxidization (Bibl. 1, p. 53). If he be correct, that means that when the vessel was fired the top part had access to a larger supply of oxygen than the lower part. How was it possible for these conditions to occur? My explanation is offered in connection with the Hou-chia Chuang ware (Section 13, pp. 26–7).

(b) Shape.—The shapes of this type of ware are much simpler than those of the plain ware. So far as I can discover, there are only two shapes, the bowl, which is the commoner shape, and a few basins. The size is also smaller in comparison with that of the plain ware.

(c) Material.—The material for making these painted vessels consists of ordinary quaternary loess and fine sand. The clay was carefully washed, since it appears homogeneous, and probably it is free from organic remains (Bibl. 6, p. 9).

(d) Thickness.—The thickness of this ware varies from 3 to 8 mm. Bowls are thinner than basins. The wall is, as a rule, very even and uniform.

(e) Method of making.—According to Dr. Andersson, the majority of the painted vessels are turned upon the potter's wheel. However, marks of the wheel have often been obliterated in the processes of scraping and burnishing. A few specimens show irregularities in shape indicating hand technique (Bibl. 1, p. 53). I think this ware is made in the same way as the painted wares of the Northern Honan group, i.e. either by ring-building or by moulding, though it is more advanced in certain respects such as surface treatment, and the frequent use of the turn-table.

(f) Surface treatment.—The surface is always smooth, sometimes with a shiny polish, which produces a darker red tone. Sometimes the surface is coated with a white slip, but it is distinct from the white ware which is also found at this site. Some vessels, especially bowls, are highly polished. The polishing was done after the vessel had been left to dry for a little time.

(g) Decoration.—The common motifs of Yang-shao are broad bands, triangles, round spots, and crossed lines (Fig. XXVI).

Section 25.—The area of this site is about 343,000 square yards. The depth of the cultural deposit is about 9 feet on the average. Only seventeen small areas corresponding to about one thousandth part of the whole site were excavated (Bibl. 1, p. 19). So the site is still far from being thoroughly explored.

Dr. Andersson asserts that the whole deposit represents a single cultural epoch of short duration, because the same sort of artifacts are found everywhere in the deposit. I agree that the Yang-shao deposit is the remains of one and the same culture, but I do not think it is of short duration. So far as I can see from the evidence of pottery finds, this site must be divided into at least two periods, Yang-shao I and Yang-shao II.

CH'IN-WANG CHAI

Section 26.—The Ch'in-wang Chai site is in the Kuang-wu district more than 100 miles east of Yang-shao. This district a few years ago was called Ho-yin, because its location is close to the southern bank of the Yellow River. About 2 miles to the south of the River a range of hills, locally known as the Kuang-wu Shan, borders the land formed by river silt. Ch'in-wang Chai is on the top of the range, at a place about 13 miles west of the Yellow River bridge on the P'ing-Han Railway, and about 8 miles north-west of the district town of Kuang-wu.

This site was found in 1921 by two servants of Dr. Andersson ; there they dug and collected more than one thousand sherds. Up to the present, however, no scientific excavation has been done on this site, therefore nothing can be said about its stratification.

This collection was studied by Dr. T. J. Arne in his *Painted Stone Age Pottery from the Province of Honan, China, 1925* (Bibl. 6). To his accurate drawings and coloured plates I am much indebted.

Section 27.—The pottery finds from Ch'in-wang Chai may be classified and described as follows :—

A. Plain Ware,   B. Decorated Ware.

A. Plain Ware.

(*a*) Colour.—The ware is brick-red, the same colour as some of the decorated ware.

(*b*) Shape.—Besides a few specimens of ordinary water-jars (Fig. XXVII), the commonest shape is a jar with a pointed base. Its usual form is shown in Fig. XXVIII. Its height is about 960 mm. and the thickness of the body, 5 mm. The lugs appear on the widest part of the vessel.

The function of this strange-shaped vessel among the home utensils can only be surmised from its shape and technical details. In the first place it could not be a cooking vessel, not only because its material and shape are unsuitable for that purpose, but also because the surface bears no marks of being burnt. Nor could it be a food or grain container, as both the lean belly and the pointed base make it unfit for that function. As its broken sherds are often found abundantly in the dwelling-sites, it is probable that it is a water-container. All the peculiarities of the vessel seem to indicate that function. The pointed base was probably designed to facilitate ready sinking. In North China to-day, a bucket with a pointed base is always attached to a well fitted with a windlass. This modern parallel has a wide mouth made specially to facilitate pouring. The narrow mouth of the prehistoric jar with its neatly made rim suggests that the vessel was probably closed with a stopper when it was filled with water. The narrow neck and the broad projecting rim make an excellent place for attaching a rope. In order to carry without effort a large jar filled with water, it would be necessary to pass a rope round the neck and then pass it through the lugs which were fixed on the lower part of the vessel. I believe that the lugs had only that special function of keeping the rope in position.

(*c*) Material.—The clay used is the same as that of the ordinary painted pottery.

(*d*) Thickness.—The wall is extremely thin, only about 3·5–5 mm., in proportion to the size of the vessel. The wall is not so uniform as that of the painted ware.

(*e*) and (*f*). Method of making and surface treatment.—How the vessel was made may be judged from the impressions on the surface. The string-impressions on the surface are regular and consist of lines which meet at the pointed base. The inner surface is uneven with

51

shallow pits. From these evidences I regard this ware as moulded. The mouth, as far as I can see, was hand-modelled separately on the turn-table. I shall discuss this special method of moulding in connection with the Hsi-yin ware (Section 50, pp. 72–4).

B. Decorated Ware.

(*a*) Colour.—The red colour of this ware is, as a rule, much lighter than that of the Yang-shao examples, although the brick-red of Yang-shao is also found. The red colour varies from light brick-red to dark brown, or violet. Not a few sherds are grey with only the surface coloured red. A kind of yellowish red is quite common.

The pottery from this site was perhaps not burnt to so high a temperature as that of the Yang-shao ware. It is estimated by Dr. P. Meyersberg that a specimen sherd from Yang-shao was burnt as high as 1,300°–1,400° C., and a specimen sherd from this site was burnt as high as 1,100°–1,200° C. (Bibl. 6, pp. 9–10). It is also clear that the degree of oxidization in kilns at this site was not so high as that at Yang-shao, since the grey colour is prevalent.

(*b*) Shape.—The common shapes are pots, jars, basins, and bowls.

(*c*) Material.—The clay is as fine as that at Yang-shao Ts'un.

(*d*) Thickness.—In this respect this ware is just the same as the Yang-shao ware.

(*e*) Method of making.—Concerning both the Yang-shao and the Ch'in-wang Chai wares, Dr. Arne asserts without hesitation that the wheel was used in the making of the red ware. His evidence is based on two characteristics of the ware, (1) flutings running parallel to the rim, (2) the fineness, thinness, and evenness of the wall (Bibl. 6, p. 11). I venture to think that these two things are not sufficient to prove that any pot is wheel-made. Some of the large pots from Ch'in-wang Chai have parallel striæ only on the top part of the vessel, and never on the body or the lower part. It is true that the decorated ware is thin and even, but these qualities are no more pronounced than in the hand-modelled wares of Northern Honan and Shansi. On the other hand, there are specimens which show signs of having been made by hand. To

52

me the most striking feature is the presence of smoothing and scraping marks on the inner surface, as well as on the outer surface. If a pot be wheel-made, there is no need to smooth or scrape the inner surface, because a scraped surface is often inferior to a wheel-made surface. Dr. Arne had not failed to notice that some vessels had broken surfaces which were produced by smoothing with an instrument.

I have proved by experiments that these pots could be made by hand. They were smoothed and finished upon a turn-table ; and that is why the parallel striæ only appear on the top part of the vessel.

(*f*) Surface treatment.—The ware with a red wash and polished surface is sometimes found at this site. The ware with a white slip is frequent ; it is similar in appearance to the real white ware of Yang-shao.

The ware without a slip has a smooth surface, which is sometimes well polished.

(*g*) Decoration.—The designs are painted on a surface which is especially prepared either by applying slip or simply by polishing. The painted designs are of a dark brownish black colour and sometimes red is used in addition. Together with the slip, a decorated zone of a vessel may thus have three colours, black, red, and white.

The motifs, as shown in Fig. XXIX, are far more complicated than those of Yang-shao. Unlike that ware, the painted rim and the triangular pattern are very rare.

Section 28.—There are some general similarities in the pottery from this site and that from Yang-shao. At both sites the water-jar with a pointed base was common. But the technique of Ch'in-wang Chai is on the whole more advanced than that of Yang-shao : the sizes are larger, the shapes more complicated, white slip is more commonly used, and the motifs are different and more varied. It is clear that the date of this site is later than that of Yang-shao.

CH'IH-KOU CHAI

Section 29.—Ch'ih-kou Chai.—The Ch'ih-kou Chai site is in the same district, Kuang-wu, as Ch'in-wang Chai, and is only about

2 miles south-west of it on the hills, known as the Kuang-wu Shan, about 9 miles west of the district town of Kuang-wu.

Dr. Arne has studied fourteen specimens from this site (Bibl. 6, p. 68), four of which are described in Dr. Andersson's *An Early Chinese Culture*. From these two sources, I have collected the following information.

Section 30.—No plain wares but only painted sherds were collected from this site.

(*a*) Colour.—The colour is either brick-red throughout, or only brick-red on the outside while the inside is grey.

(*b*) Shape.—Judging by the few specimens, some shapes from this site are the same as those of Ch'in-wang Chai, though I believe that they are smaller in size.

(*c*) Material.—The clay is the same as that of the decorated ware of Ch'in-wang Chai.

(*d*) Thickness.—The ware is even and the average thickness about 5 mm.

(*e*) Method of making.—The method of making is the same as that of the decorated ware from Ch'in-wang Chai.

(*f*) Surface treatment.—The surface is polished. White slip is sometimes used.

(*g*) Decoration.—The motifs are very similar to those of Ch'in-wang Chai (Fig. XXX). But, as may be seen in Fig. XXX, 3 and 4, there is a new saw-tooth pattern which is not found either at Ch'in-wang Chai or Yang-shao Ts'un. The designs of Fig. XXX, 3, are also peculiar to this site.

Pu-chao Chai

Section 31.—Pu-chao Chai.—The Pu-chao Chai site is only about 3 miles west of Yang-shao Ts'un. It was found during the excavation of Yang-shao in 1921, but it has never been properly explored.

Only six nearly complete vessels have been described by Dr. Andersson and Dr. Arne. Most of the following information was

54

gathered from their works (Bibl. 1 and 6), some from my own personal observation.

Section 32.—No painted ware has been found at this site. We shall have to deal with only one kind of ware : Plain Coarse.

(*a*) Colour.—The ware is mostly grey, sometimes brown.

(*b*) Shape.—The shapes are much more varied than those of Yang-shao Ts'un, Ch'in-wang Chai, or Ch'ih-kou Chai. The *li* is quite common (Fig. XXXI) and one steaming vessel, known as the *yen* (Fig. XXXII), was also found.

(*c*) Material.—The material consists of clay usually mixed with sand. The ware looks much coarser than the painted ware of Yang-shao.

(*d*) Thickness.—The wall is not uniform or even. In a single sherd the thickness may vary from 2 to 4 mm., 2 to 7 mm., 5 to 9 mm., or 6 to 10 mm.

(*e*) and (*f*). Method of making and surface treatment.—There are clear and deep string-impressions on the outer surface of the *li*. When some part of the wall of the *li* is as thin as 3 to 4 mm., these impressions may also appear in negative on the inside of the vessel, though less distinct than on the outside. These impressions on the inside serve as strong evidence against the theory that such wares were fashioned by hand on a bed of matting (Bibl. 1, p. 28) ; by that method the impressions of the matting would be produced only on the outside of the vessel. In my opinion, this ware is moulded. Some vessels show regular striæ on the rim, indicating that they were finished upon a turn-table (Fig. XXXIII).

This ware is quite similar to the coarse plain ware of Yang-shao, and I propose to date this site as contemporary with Yang-shao II.

OTHER WESTERN HONAN SITES NOW BEING EXPLORED

Section 33.—Ch'ên Kou.—This site is situated 6 miles north-west of the district town of the Kuang-wu Hsien, on the heights known as the Kuang-wu Shan. It was excavated in 1934 by the Archæological Society of Honan, under the auspices of the Academia Sinica.

The painted wares from this site have motifs similar to those of Ch'in-wang Chai. There seems to be some relation between the shape and the design ; certain designs often appear on certain shapes. The cooking vessel *ting* is found at this site, and also the water-jar with a pointed base like that of Ch'in-wang Chai (Bibl. 10, p. 6).

Judging by this scanty information it may be inferred that this site is contemporary with Ch'in-wang Chai site in the same district.

Section 34.—Ch'ing T'ai.—The Ch'ing T'ai site is about $2\frac{1}{2}$ miles west of the district town of Kuang-wu, and north of the Shan-jan River. It was excavated in 1934 by the Archæological Society of Honan under the auspices of the Academia Sinica.

Very large *ting* and water-jars with a pointed base are found at this site and no *li*. A beaker of black pottery very much like that from Lung-shan is also found. The painted designs are of the same type as those of Ch'ên Kou, but some are more complicated (Bibl. 10, p. 5).

Judging by the large size of the vessels and the influence of the Black Pottery culture, I believe this site is later than Ch'ên Kou.

Section 35.—T'a P'o.—The village T'a P'o is about 7 miles north-west of the district town of Kuang-wu, right on the south bank of the Yellow River. The site is only about 300 yards east of the village ; only a part of it remains, the other having been washed away by the River. It was excavated in 1934 by the Archæological Society of Honan under the auspices of the Academia Sinica.

The Red Pottery from this site has a painted rim in black like the simple Ta-lai Tien designs. But in some specimens the inside of the rim is also decorated. A strangely shaped *ting*, oval in section, is found at this site (Bibl. 10, p. 8). This is the most primitive type of red ware found in Western Honan, and I believe it is earlier than any of the other sites in that district.

Section 36.—From the survey of the pottery of the seven sites in Western Honan we may summarize their main features and arrange them in a chronological order.

In his article *An Early Chinese Culture*, 1923 (Bibl. 1, pp. 47–68), Dr. Andersson put together the finds from three sites in Western

Honan and decided that they all belong to the same culture which he called by the name Yang-shao. In my opinion, it is correct to include the Ch'ih-kou Chai site in this cultural group as the painted pottery is more or less identical. But Pu-chao Chai cannot be included for several reasons. The pottery remains at Pu-chao Chai are of a different type from those of the other two sites. Though the distance between Yang-shao Ts'un and Pu-chao Chai is not great (3 miles), no discovery has yet been made to connect the two sites, and there seems to be no justification for doing so.

Yang-shao Ts'un and Pu-chao Chai are near each other in the Mien-ch'ih District. Ch'ih-kou Chai, Ch'in-wang Chai, Ch'ên Kou, Ch'ing T'ai, and T'a P'o are near each other in the Kuang-wu District. The distance between these two districts is about 100 miles. In six of these seven sites there is plenty of decorated pottery; only at the Pu-chao Chai site no such kind of pottery has been found.

As I have mentioned, the earliest type of painted pottery is found at T'a P'o; it is, therefore, reasonable to regard it as the earliest site in Western Honan.

The fact that the colours of the Ch'in-wang Chai and the Ch'ih-kou Chai wares are uniform indicates that the potters had advanced knowledge of the craft. The Yang-shao ware is not so uniform in colour, and there are a few pieces which have been burnt to a very high temperature, higher than necessary for ordinary earthenware. The shapes of the plain ware from all the sites are, as a rule, more varied than those of the decorated ware. The greatest variety of shapes is found at the Pu-chao Chai site, where only plain pottery was discovered. As regards decorated ware only, the Ch'in-wang Chai site has a greater number of shapes than Yang-shao. The material of the Pu-chao Chai ware is coarser than that of the wares of the other six sites. So far no evidence of the use of the wheel has been found at any of the seven sites.

At Ch'in-wang Chai and Ch'ih-kou Chai the method of surface treatment had reached a higher stage than it had reached at Yang-shao T'sun. The Pu-chao Chai potters paid little attention to the surface. The designs of Ch'in-wang Chai, Ch'ên Kou, and also Ch'ih-kou Chai are more complicated than those of Yang-shao Ts'un. Among the motifs of Ch'in-wang Chai, there are only a few simple ones which are similar to those of Yang-shao Ts'un.

The Yang-shao ware must be taken as earlier than that of Ch'in-wang Chai, because its colour, shape, decoration, and techniques show more primitive characters. Judged by the same criteria, the Ch'ih-kou Chai ware, though consisting at present of only a few pieces, may be regarded as contemporary with Ch'in-wang Chai.

Now let us come to the problem of relative date of Pu-chao Chai with regard to the other sites. Dr. Andersson has taken it to be an earlier stage of the Yang-shao Culture, because painted ceramics are absent. But I regard it as later than all the other six sites, for the following reasons. The technique of the moulded ware at Pu-chao Chai had reached a higher stage than the moulded ware of the other sites. The shapes of Pu-chao Chai ware are more varied and complicated than those of the other sites. Pots, shaped like bronze *li* and *yen*, show affinity with the Bronze Age. The absence of painted pottery and the prevalence of grey pottery indicates a type of culture similar to Ta-lai Tien II in Northern Honan which represents a late stage of the Black Pottery culture.

Therefore, the chronological sequence of the seven sites of Western Honan may be arranged as follows :—

(1) T'a P'o.
(2) Yang-shao I.
(3) Ch'in-wang Chai, Ch'ih-kou Chai and Ch'ên Kou.
(4) Ch'ing T'ai.
(5) Yang-shao II and Pu-chao Chai.

CHAPTER III

THE SHANTUNG GROUP

Section 37.—This group includes the pottery finds from four sites, viz. Lung-shan, Liang-ch'êng, Fêng-huang T'ai, and An-shang Ts'un.

LUNG-SHAN
(*Ch'êng-tzŭ Yai*)

Section 38.—The Ch'êng-tzŭ Yai site was discovered by myself in 1928, and it is the first site of the Black Pottery culture ever discovered in China. My report on the discovery of this site was published in 1930 (Bibl. 29), and that on the pottery in 1934 (Bibl. 31). This site is situated near a terrace of the Wu-yüan River, about 25 miles east of Chi-nan, the capital of the Shantung province. As this site is just opposite the town of Lung-shan, it is often called the Lung-shan site, and the Black Pottery culture, the Lung-shan culture.

The top of the Ch'êng-tzŭ Yai mound is 6–18 feet above the surrounding ground. The settlement was built on a natural terrace about 3 feet high and the cultural deposit is no less than 16 feet deep on the average.

The whole deposit consists of two cultural layers, the lower contains remains of the Black Pottery culture and the upper layer is characterized by grey pottery (Bibl. 30, p. 24). The cultural deposit of the lower layer, or the first period, is not so evenly distributed as that of the upper layer, or the second period. It seems to me that the population of the first period was not so dense as that of the second period. The boundary of the settlement is clearly marked by the remains of a wall which was built in the first period and repaired in the second period (Bibl. 33, p. 28) ; only inside this rampart are stratified remains to be found.

Between these two cultural layers at a depth of 5–6 feet is a thin layer (about 1½ feet thick) of sand and silt containing few artifacts. This scarcity of artifacts in this intermediate layer suggests that after this site was abandoned by the Black Pottery people, there was a period during which it was uninhabited. When the people who used grey pottery came, they found no buildings left intact, not even the colossal wall surrounding the site. Judging by the thickness of their cultural deposit these users of grey pottery must have remained at this site about the same length of time as the Black Pottery people.

There are not more than one hundred specimens of which the shapes can easily be ascertained. The sherds, especially those of the black ware, are very fragmentary.

The pottery finds of the upper layer belong to the Chou period. Pottery of the historic period is beyond the scope of this thesis, so I propose to describe it only briefly, and I shall not include it in the formal classification of the pottery from this site.

Section 39.—The pottery finds from Lung-shan II may be classified and described as follows :—

Type A.—The colour is mainly grey, though the tone changes from silver grey to dark bluish grey. The fracture shows that the colour is, as a rule, the same throughout, and therefore the heat of the kiln must have been scientifically controlled.

As in the production of the Shang-Yin ware, the " yin-yao " method (or that by which the kiln is made to imbibe moisture) was practised, and evidently to a great extent, as there are no red wares but only grey wares found in this layer. The large water-jars with a rounded base with or without ears are common (Fig. LXVII). The clay is coarse but uniform in quality. It must have been prepared by some refining process. The ware is uniformly even and the average thickness is about 6–7 mm. The beater and pad method was widely used in this period. The marks of the beater are much finer and shallower (Fig. LXVII) than those on the Shang-Yin ware. They are regularly arranged and appear sometimes quite similar to the marks of the mould. The untouched surface is the special feature of this period. By untouched, or raw, I mean the surface produced by beating, or moulding without any smoothing or polishing by hand.

Type B.—Extra coarse ware. This is a kind of coarse grey ware made chiefly in the form of the *li* (Fig. XXXIV, 24). It is moulded, and the average thickness is about 7 mm. The surface is untouched and rough.

Type C. Fine ware.—This is a class of wheel-made ware. The size is usually small and the shapes are dishes (Fig. XXXIV, 3), bowls (Fig. XXXIV, 5), *min* (Fig. XXXIV, 12), and *tou* (Fig. XXXIV, 13). The *tou* is found in such large quantities that the excavators called the upper layer the *tou*-containing layer. During the two seasons of work no less than 500 *tou* were unearthed. The material should be classified as coarse, but the amount of sand seems to have been added in a constant proportion. The average thickness is about 6–10 mm., and the surface is untouched, but not rough, just like the surface of any wheel-made ware.

There is no decorated ware belonging to this cultural layer. But at other sites of the Chou period in Shantung I have found pots with incised or stamped ornaments, though the amount of this decorated ware in comparison with the plain ware is negligible.

Section 40.—The pottery finds from Lung-shan I may be classified and described as follows :—

A. Plain Ware,   B. Decorated Ware.
    1. Coarse, *a* and *b*.
    2. Fine.

A 1. Plain Coarse Ware.—This ware may be further divided into two sub-classes : A 1*a*, cooking vessels, and A 1*b*, other kinds of vessels.

(*a*) Colour.—Grey and black are both common in this class of ware, while white and red are less common.

(*b*) Shape.—Large basins and three-footed vessels with hollow legs are the usual shapes.

These shapes (Fig. XXXIV, 27, 28) are very much akin to bronze

61

shapes. That means to say they are either the forerunners or the descendants of the Bronze Age.

The use of lids became popular in this period.

No *li* were found in this period, though they occur in the layer corresponding to the Chou period. Some of the *ting* legs are decorated with the motif somewhat like a human mask, which the excavators called " the devil's face ".

(*c*) Material.—The cooking vessels (A 1*a*) are made either of a very gritty ware or of white ware, while the other kinds of vessels (A 1*b*) are made of coarse clay, which is not properly washed.

(*d*) Thickness.—The cooking vessels (A 1*a*) are always made with thin and uniform walls. The average thickness is about 5 mm. But the other clay vessels (A 1*b*) are rough, uneven, and clumsy.

(*e*) and (*f*) Method of making and surface treatment.—The small vessels are hand-made, a few basins of rough ware are moulded and all the other vessels are wheel-made.

Small vessels were simply smoothed with the wet hand and no further treatment was applied. The cooking vessels were smoothed with the wet hand, but the surface thus produced is still rather rough. Some wheel-made pots were not smoothed at all, and the raw surface was kept. The moulded ware has the impressions of the string mould on the surface. These impressions are peculiar to this site ; they are horizontal instead of vertical as those on moulded ware of the sites in Honan, and it is evident that they were produced by a more primitive method. By making several experiments, I have finally come to the conclusion that the moulding process was probably as follows : (1) make a round base ; (2) build the wall by coiling ; after a height of about 2 inches is reached, wind a continuous line of string round the wall ; (3) continue to build the wall by coiling and to wind the string round it until the required height is attained ; (4) wait till the pot is nearly dry, then take off the string.

In this way a pot with horizontal string marks is produced. I found it much easier to fashion a large open basin with the aid of the string than by the ordinary ring-building method. In this process, which

I propose to call string-moulding, it is possible to use the clay in a very soft state, and the inner surface can easily be pressed and smoothed without destroying the shape.

A 2. Plain Fine Ware.

(a) Colour.—The most common colour is black, grey is less common ; brick-red, yellow, and white are rare.

On the surface, all black wares look the same, but if the fracture is carefully examined, a difference in colouring may be observed. One kind of black ware is not uniform in colour, i.e. the colour of the surface is different from that of the core, which is either red or grey. There is another kind of ware which is black throughout. The excavators call it the typical black ware. The ware with only a black surface under which there is a grey or red core is called the pseudo-black ware, which is, as a rule, thicker than the typical Lung-shan ware.

The red ware is usually red throughout and it is rarely found with a grey or black core. That is because the red sherds are always thin, and have been thoroughly baked.

(b) Shape.—So far as I can see there are certainly more than thirty shapes in the plain fine ware of Lung-shan I. The common ones are cup, bowl, beaker, basin, jar, *min*, and *ting* (Fig. XXXIV, 1, 2, 4, 4–12, 14–25). The shapes are graceful, and I believe they are some of the most beautiful shapes among the ancient wares in the Far East.

The shapes of small vessels are especially attractive. Some of them seem to be too small to serve any practical purpose, but these small sizes are fairly common. They could not have been mere ornaments. As they were found in a dwelling site, they are not funerary objects. They were probably containers of valuable liquids or precious foodstuffs.

(c) Material.—The preparation of clay reached its highest stage of development during this period. The clay may be divided into two classes, fine and extraordinarily fine ; the former was produced by washing and the latter by levigation, which is simply repeated washing.

63

In the second class no sand or any kind of foreign material can be found even when magnified ten times.

At this site we find such a clear distinction between the gritty and the fine wares, that we can tell the one from the other at a glance.

(*d*) Thickness.—I found some black sherds which are less than 1 mm. in thickness, almost as thin as egg-shell. The average thickness is about 3 mm. and the wall is very even.

(*e*) Method of making.—Some of the small vessels, such as cups and bowls, are modelled by hand but most of this class of wares are wheel-made. The characteristic features of wheel technique are evident : all over the body there are horizontal parallel striæ (Fig. XXXV) ; on the outer surface, there are ridges and furrows also horizontal and parallel (Fig. XXXV) ; the wall is uniformly even (Fig. XXXIV, 23) ; on the interior of the base a spiral is sometimes visible ; the shape is often globular ; a transverse section cut through the body at any height is in the form of a perfect circle ; the highest edge of the rim is sharp and clean and on a plane which is parallel to that of the base (Fig. XXXIV, 1–23).

The fineness and evenness of the ware, the accuracy of the shape, all testify to the high stage of the wheel-technique. It is no exaggeration to say that the making of earthenware in China had reached its climax at this period, and no potter before or after has ever produced any ware as perfect as the Lung-shan ware.

(*f*) Surface treatment.—The surface of the hand-modelled vessels is not even, but fairly smooth. The wheel-made ware has a surface carefully burnished on the wheel. The glossy surface is sometimes like blackened leather, or black lacquer. I have learned through experiments that the burnishing must have been done when the ware is nearly dry. The instrument for burnishing may be a pebble, a tooth, or any object which has a hard and glossy surface. In comparison with the method of polishing by hand with the same sort of instruments, burnishing on the wheel is certainly a wonderful innovation in the ceramic art. A work which requires hours to polish by hand can be done in a few minutes by burnishing on the wheel. The burnished

64

surface can easily be detected by the presence of parallel striæ, which are finer and shallower than those produced by the throwing process, and are quite different from the marks produced by polishing.

B. Decorated Ware.

In the decorated ware, except a few specimens, the colour, shape and technical characteristics are the same as those of the plain fine ware. The few exceptions are cooking vessels which have the same characteristics of manufacture as the plain coarse ware made by means of the wheel.

No painted ware has been found at this site. But other kinds of decorated ware are present, though they are comparatively rare : the decoration is carried out either by treating the surface, or by attaching decorative accessories to the pot. Marks on the surface are often made on the wheel such as a few deep and sharp furrows, or a band of parallel lines. In the pseudo-black ware, the surface is sometimes cut with cross-hatched lines, though this is rare. On the rim, lid, or body, miniature ears and knobs are often present, especially in the typical black ware. Knobs on the lid may appear in the form of a bird's head with hooked bill and bulging eyes very much like those on bronze vessels. On the handle of the jug with three hollow legs and an elongated lip (Fig. XXXIV, 28) four knobs marking the four corners of the handle often appear.

Section 41.—The finds from the two layers of Lung-shan are so different from each other that we must admit the existence of an interval of time between the earliest and latest periods. Stone tools were found in both layers, but the *li* and the *tou* were found only in the upper layer while the prototype of the *tou* (Fig. XXXIV, 14) was found in the lower layer. Oracle bones were found in both layers, but those from the lower layer have been prepared by simple processes (Bibl. 34, pp. 88–9).

The most significant feature of this site is the presence of the shiny black ware made by highly developed wheel-technique, the surface treatment of which is so characteristic that one may recognize it at a glance.

The upper layer is identified as the remains of the Kingdom of T'an, corresponding to about 1122 (from the beginning of the Chou) to 684 B.C.

The Black Pottery from the lower layer (Lung-shan I) is similar in almost every respect to the Black Pottery of Hou Kang II in Honan, and there is no doubt in my mind that these two layers are of contemporary date.

LIANG-CH'ÊNG

Section 42.—The Liang-ch'êng site is about 5 miles from the sea and 15 miles north-east of the district town of Jih-chao, and about $\frac{1}{2}$ mile west of the large village Liang-ch'êng. It was found by Mr. Wang Hsiang and Mr. Ch'i Yen-p'ei, members of the Academia Sinica, during their archæological exploration in the spring of 1933. This site was excavated in the summer of 1936 under the leadership of Mr. Liang Ssŭ-yung.

Two areas of the site have been excavated, the names of which are the Mound, named after the high mound at the centre of the site, and Wa-wu Ts'un to the south-east of the Mound, named after the village near which it is situated. The Mound area contains only Black Pottery and the cultural layer is only about 3–5 feet deep. The Wa-wu Ts'un area is deeper—about 9 feet on the average. During the excavations more than fifty tombs have been found. The funerary objects are mainly black-ware pots.

Section 43.—The pottery finds from this site may be classified and described as follows :—

A. Plain,   B. Decorated.
   1. Coarse,
   2. Fine.

A 1. Plain Coarse Ware.

(a) Colour.—There are two common colours, black and red ; white ware is also found in small quantities. The black gritty ware is often black only on the surface while the core is red.

66

(*b*) Shape.—The three-footed vessels of red or white ware are common. Such shapes often have lids (Fig. XXXVI, *e, f*) belonging to them, though the vessel and the lid are seldom found together.

(*c*) Material.—The clay of this ware is invariably mixed with sand, the grains of which are not uniform in size. This is one of the peculiarities of this ware. The cooking vessels of light brick-red colour are made of a coarser material than that of the black gritty vessels. The white ware is of the same kind of material as that of Lung-shan, though the sand in it is less uniform in quality. The white ware is hard, showing that it has been fired at a high temperature.

(*d*) Thickness.—The sherds are uniformly even and the average thickness is about 5 mm.

(*e*) Method of making.—This ware is wheel-made, though the small accessories, such as legs and handles, are often made by hand. The hollow legs of cooking vessels are on the other hand made on the wheel. To fashion a hollow cone on the wheel requires great skill. It is evident that the wheel-technique had reached an advanced stage.

(*f*) Surface treatment.—The surface of cooking vessels of black gritty ware and white ware is only smoothed with the wet hand. A white slip is often applied to the surface of the brick-red ware, and then polished, thus producing a smooth and slippery coating. Like the cooking vessels at any other site, the surfaces often show signs of being blackened by fire.

A 2. Plain Fine Ware.

(*a*) Colour.—Black is the usual colour, while dark grey is less common. Judging by colour alone, there are two kinds of black ware, the typical black, and the pseudo-black ware. The typical black ware is black throughout, though the surface, being polished, often has a darker shade. On some parts of the inner surface of a certain number of sherds and complete pots of typical black ware, I have noticed a thin whitish layer. It is not a slip or wash, it is simply a discoloration due to the action of water. The pseudo-black ware has generally a thicker wall than the typical black. The black layer of the pseudo-black

67

ware is only surface deep, rarely more than 1 mm. thick. The average thickness of the wall is about 5 mm. or more, and the surface layer may flake off entirely and expose the grey core.

(*b*) Shape.—The shapes (Fig. XXXVI, *a–h*) are very similar to those of Lung-shan. Certain characteristic details of the Black Pottery period, such as the sharply bent rims, the horizontally set handles, and the bowl and dish-covers are well represented among the wares of this site.

(*c*) Material.—Like that of the Lung-shan site, the clay is well prepared presumably by levigation or similar process. The material of the *ting*, and also of the small vessels is as fine as the finest material of the modern wares, such as that used for making tea pots and wine jars.

(*d*) Thickness.—On the whole, the ware is extraordinarily fine and even, and the average thickness is about 3 mm.

(*e*) Method of making.—As in the Lung-shan ware, we find the same evidence that this type of Black Pottery is undoubtedly wheel-made.

(*f*) Surface treatment.—The surface was burnished on the wheel when the ware was nearly dry. Very fine parallel lines are thus produced. The basins were burnished both on the outside and the inside, while small vessels or vessels with a small mouth were only burnished on the outer surface. Through wear and tear the shiny surface may be destroyed, and the appearance become dull.

B. Decorated Ware.

This ware is decorated in two ways, by treating the surface, or by adding ornamental accessories. (1) Cross-hatched lines appear on the shoulder or on the body and form an ornamental pattern. The deep furrows intentionally made by the action of the wheel are also for the purpose of decoration. (2) Miniature knobs and ears to the number of four or more are placed near the rim ; knobs are placed on the lid, and on the handle to mark the junction with the body. The knobs on the lids are often made in a decorative form such as a bird's head

68

(Fig. XXXVI, *f*) similar to others from Lung-shan. The *ting* leg in the form of the " devil's face " is also found (Fig. XXXVI, *h*).

In other aspects of technique it is the same as the plain fine ware, A 2.

Section 44.—The Liang-ch'êng finds are similar to those of Lung-shan I, except that no shell or bone implements, no animal bones or oracle bones have been found. The typical features of Black Pottery culture such as the *ting* with the legs ornamented with the devil's face, and spouted vessels, are all found at this site. But not a single *li* has been discovered. There is no grey pottery in the proper Black Pottery layer. Among the stone tools, there are axes, adzes, chisels, arrow-heads, and semilunar knives, all like those of Lung-shan.

Judging from its appearance, the Liang-ch'êng ware seems not to be so well made as the Lung-shan ware, especially as regards the burnishing of the surface.

This site contains only wares made by Black Pottery technique and there is no moulded ware in the proper cultural layers. The wheel-technique had reached such a high stage of development that even the smallest vessels were wheel-made.

The pottery finds from this site show that its date is contemporary with that of Lung-shan.

OTHER SHANTUNG SITES NOW BEING EXPLORED

Section 45.—Fêng-huang T'ai.—In the winter of 1932, during my archæological tour in the southern districts of Shantung, I made some discoveries at a mound, known as the Fêng-huang T'ai, or Phœnix Terrace. The Terrace is situated a few hundred yards north-east of Lin-ch'êng village in T'êng Hsien and about 2 miles north of Lin-ch'êng Station on the Tientsin Pukow Railway. The top of the mound is flat. Its area is about 100 square feet. At the centre of the flat area, there is a tomb with its stones and bricks partly exposed. Within about 40 feet from the tomb, the cultural soil is exposed by the action of rain. Ancient artifacts of pottery, stone, and bone were found upon the surface. Among the potsherds I picked up coarse and fine

69

black wares of the Lung-shan type, though not so good as regards technique. Numerous pieces of *li* sherds and sherds of the grey pottery of the Chou type were collected, but not a single piece of the typical Lung-shan ware was found. After I had brought these samples back to Chi-nan and compared them with the Lung-shan finds, I came to the conclusion that the date of the Phœnix Terrace must be later than Lung-shan I.

Section 46.—An-shang Ts'un.—In the spring of 1933, some bronze vessels were found by the farmers at a site near An-shang Ts'un about 30 miles north of Lin-ch'êng, also in T'êng Hsien. In the same year the site was excavated by the Academia Sinica. Besides pottery, bronze, stone, and bone artifacts were found. Among the pottery finds there is no typical Lung-shan ware, though there are plenty of wares of an inferior Lung-shan type. The string-impressed ware is the commonest type, especially in the shape of *li*. In my opinion, the finds are exactly the same as those from the Phœnix Terrace.

Section 47.—Summing up the results of the study of the Shantung Group, I have arranged the various sites in the following chronological order :

(1) Lung-shan I and Liang-ch'êng.
(2) An-shang Ts'un and Fêng-huang T'ai.
(3) Lung-shan II.

Chapter IV

THE SHANSI GROUP

Section 48.—This group consists of the pottery finds from two sites, Hsi-yin Ts'un and Ching Ts'un.

Hsi-yin Ts'un

Section 49.—The Hsi-yin Ts'un site is situated just inside the great bend of the Yellow River in the Shansi Province, within Hsia Hsien. In this district there stands a temple attributed to the Great Yü, the founder of the Hsia dynasty, and certain sites are popularly thought to be the tombs of his descendants and ministers.

The area of this site was no less than 500,000 square yards (Bibl. 13, p. 34). Dr. Li selected and dug only a small area, which covers twelve " squares ", each of which measures about 43 square feet. The whole excavated area was about 516 square feet (ibid., p. 7).

Within this small area, a collection was made of more than sixty large packing cases of finds, mainly potsherds with very few bone, stone, and other artifacts. The pottery was very fragmentary, some sherds were smaller than a finger nail, and not a single complete pot was found.

Section 50.—The pottery finds from this site may be classified and described as follows :—

A. Plain Ware,   B. Decorated Ware.
    1. Coarse,
    2. Fine.

A 1. Plain Coarse Ware.

(a) Colour.—The colour of this type of ware may be divided into two main categories, grey and red. The grey varies in tone, but is

71

usually brownish. The red is a bright warm colour. But the red sherds are quite commonly red only on the outside while the inside is grey.

(*b*) Shape.—The shapes of the grey ware are mainly pots (Fig. XXXVII, 8, 10, 11, 17, 19, 35), some of which have bulging sides, and some straight walls forming an oblique angle with the base. There are a few shallow dishes and basins. The only shape of the red ware is the water-jar (Fig. XXXVII, 36–8) with a pointed base like that of Yang-shao Ts'un in Western Honan.

(*c*) Material.—The material is not homogeneous, grains of sand as large as 2 mm. in diameter are often found in the fracture. The material of the red ware is of a finer quality.

(*d*) Thickness.—The average is about 12 mm., while the extremes vary from 3 to 21 mm. The red ware is always thinner than the grey.

(*e*) Method of making.—There is no evidence of the wheel-technique, but it is clear that the turn-table has been used in the process of ring-building and for the purpose of finishing the rim. This type of ware is made chiefly by ring-building. The evidence of this method is twofold, the presence of ridges on the inner surface, and the tendency to break along lines parallel to the rim.

In the ring-building method the pot is formed from the base upwards. But there is an exception in this class. The water-jar with a pointed base was built from the top downwards. It was made in several sections, and every new section was joined to the previous one until the required length was reached. The pointed base was made by squeezing and twisting the last one or two sections so as to make the walls join. This explains why we may find volutes like those of a snail shell inside the pointed base. The mouth was made separately on the turn-table and fitted on to the jar.

In making the water-jar by ring-building, the aid of a mould was required. I shall discuss this problem in the next paragraphs.

(*f*) Surface Treatment.—Smoothing and scraping are the common processes. A few thick coarse wares of a highly gritty nature show a peculiar method of surface treatment : the outer surface is covered with a thick red slip, and polished to such a degree that it becomes

72

glossy. The surface of the grey ware, except a few small vessels, is covered over entirely with groups of string-impressions, more or less parallel, some running vertically and some diagonally. Sometimes these impressed lines are crossed on the upper part of the vessel by incised horizontal lines. Sometimes these horizontal lines are deepened into grooves. There are also a few specimens the surface of which is covered with wavy bands in relief or small circular disks also in relief. With the exception of cooking vessels, pots with string-impressions have a smooth inner surface which bears signs of having been produced by hand. The string-impressions are sometimes smoothed down and destroyed, especially those on the regions near the rim or on the base.

The string-impressions on the red-ware water-jars are different from those on the grey ware. They show the following characteristics : (1) The direction of the impressed lines is more or less constant, making an angle of about 45–60 degrees with the rim. (2) There are no impressed lines on the mouth. (3) Only at the pointed base do these lines intersect and form a trelliswork pattern. (4) The length of a single line seldom exceeds 8 cm. (5) Judging from its impression, the string must have been fine and the strands loosely knit. (6) The impressed lines are fairly uniform in width. They are all fine without any coarse lines mixed with them. Sometimes they look like threads.

Judging by these characteristics, I believe these string-impressions were made by means of some method of moulding. I have mentioned the string-mould in connection with the coarse ware found at Lung-shan I in Shantung (Section 40, pp. 61-3). So far as I can see, this is also string-moulding, but slightly different from that of Lung-shan. Instead of a single string, a number of strings laid parallel and arranged in a band was bound round the newly made section of the jar in order to strengthen it. This is necessary because the jar is tall ; the first section of about 1 foot high must be strong enough to bear the weight of the second. By this method, the various characteristics of this ware mentioned above may be produced. The impressed lines are all in the same direction, because the string-mould was applied in a constant direction. As the mouth was made separately on the turn-table by means of an entirely different method, string-impressions were of course absent from that part of the vessel. At the pointed base, where the strings were bound round several times in order to get the pointed base into proper shape, intersection of lines would naturally occur. In the process of moulding, the inner surface was pressed with the flattened fingers of one hand ; the impressed lines on the other surface could not, therefore, be longer than the fore part of the hand, the length of which is about 8 cm. The fineness and uniformity of the impressions may be explained by the simple reason that some fine and uniform strings were employed in the moulding.

A 2. Plain Fine Ware.

(*a*) Colour.—The colour of this ware is generally brick-red. Pinkish or brownish red is rare. There is also grey in various tones, tending to become dark, sometimes nearly black. White, yellow and dark brown are also found.

(*b*) Shape.—Bowls (Fig. XXXVII, 39–60, 63–6) and basins (Fig. XXXVII, 1–7, 9, 12–16, 18) are the common shapes. Jars of variously shaped walls are also found in this ware (Fig. XXXVII, 20–34, 61–2, 67–8). The round-based bowl is not found at Hsi-yin, but there is the peculiar carinated bowl (Fig. XXXVII, 61).

(*c*) Material.—The clay is fine and well washed.

(*d*) Thickness.—The average thickness is about 6 mm., while the extremes vary from 3 to 13 mm.

(*e*) Method of making.—The bowls of Hsi-yin were made by a process which was more elaborate than that used to make large vessels such as basins and pots. The process was as follows : (1) to make a bowl by ring-building, (2) to smooth the surface with the wet hand, or, as was often done, apply to the surface a layer of red slip, (3) when the vessel was nearly dry, to polish the surface to a shiny brightness. This may be the final stage but sometimes the polished bowl was painted with black pigment.

The large vessels of this ware were made by ring-building. But the finishing process was done on a turn-table. The parallel striæ left on the rim by this instrument are similar to those left by the wheel technique. But the striation is limited to the rim, never appearing on any other parts of the pot. The purpose of finishing a pot on a turn-table is to make a neat rim. The rim of a large vessel, especially a cooking vessel, has necessarily to be well defined and finished in order that a cover may be fitted over it without leaving a gap.

(f) Surface treatment.—The outer surface was subjected to the following processes : (1) The surface was first roughly smoothed with the wet hand, or with a spatula. Marks of this instrument can be seen sometimes on the lower part of the vessel, but always on the outer surface and rarely on the inner surface. It was perhaps a piece of bamboo, wood, or more likely gourd rind. Its length, as far as can be judged by these marks, is about 20–30 mm. (2) Only a small proportion of this ware was polished after the smoothing process. The surface of basins was rarely polished. (3) Bowls were often covered with a red wash before polishing. The highly polished surface of the slip sometimes flakes off. It is not due to decomposition, but to a physical cause, i.e. the difference in the coefficient of expansion of the dense surface layer and the inner layer. In a few instances white slip was used. The purpose of using slip was not only to prepare the surface for painting, but also to increase the impermeability of the surface.

The inner surface was mainly smoothed by the wet hand. Creases and joins were smoothed down by moving the hand to and fro. The characteristic marks of this action are clearly visible on the inner surface. Marks of the spatula are as rare on the inner surface as marks of the hand on the outer surface. The inner surface of the bowls was just as well finished as the outer surface.

Except bowls, the lowest zone near the base of the vessel was not so carefully smoothed and polished as the upper part.

B. Decorated Ware.

Painting is the only kind of decoration that we find at Hsi-yin Ts'un. The technique of the painted ware is the same as that of the

75

plain fine ware, A 2. It should be noted that the wares are small and finely made ; the shapes are limited to bowls and basins, but the bowls are in the majority. The average thickness is about 6 mm., while the extremes vary from 3 to 9 mm. We need now only discuss the painted decoration.

The painted designs were mostly executed on a well prepared surface, rarely on a string-impressed surface, which is obviously unsuitable. The rim, being the most conspicuous part of the vessel, is usually painted with a band. The upper part, though not so often painted as the rim, is the only place on which are found the decorative patterns. The lower part, the base, and the inner side of the vessel were left plain.

The painted colours are mainly black ; red and yellow are extremely rare.

The pigments used must have been thinly mixed with a solvent so that the colours would be easily absorbed into the clay. I have, however, noticed places where the black pigments had flaked off from the surface, and left clearly defined marks. This is because the pigments used were too thick, and consequently were not entirely absorbed. The dense surface of the painted area has a greater coefficient of expansion than the plain area ; consequently it cracks and flakes off just like the highly polished slip of the plain fine ware.

Judging by the quality of the strokes, the designs must have been executed by expert hands : the broad lines and bands show much strength and firmness and have sharp ends and well-defined edges. Curves were done with a single sweep.

As regard the painting implements, the brush was certainly one of them. The subtleties of the designs (Fig. XXXVIII) give us some general idea about the brush. The ends of the vertical as well as the horizontal lines (Fig. XXXVIII, 5, 25, 36, 51) show that the brush had a point just like a modern Chinese writing brush ; it could take a large quantity of ink, and so several strokes could be drawn with one brushful. It seems to have been a brush of hair. Such a brush would produce the characteristic designs of Hsi-yin : the triangle (Fig.

76

XXXVIII, 13), the crescent (Fig. XXXVIII, 37–8), and curved or crossed lines (Fig. XXXVIII, 2, 4, 39, 40–6, 51, 52). Straight lines are rare and the groups of lines running side by side are rarely exactly parallel (Fig. XXXVIII, 44). There are no circles. Certain broad motifs were presumably not done with a brush but with some implement like a ball of wool. One of the favourite motifs is the round spot (Fig. XXXVIII, 22–4, 28–36) which would have been made by pressing the fully charged ball on to the surface. The turn-table was also used in the process of painting. The broad band on the rim (Fig. XXXVIII, 1, 14, 44) of the bowls and basins must have been painted with a ball on the turn-table.

The motifs of Hsi-yin are geometric, and they are on a symmetrical basis. The symmetry is not only evident in the arrangement of the motifs themselves but also in the composition of the blank spaces between the motifs. The blank spaces are quite often larger than the area covered by the motifs ; and their shapes and disposition are no less attractive than the painted motifs.

Section 51.—Hsi-yin Ts'un is a typical dwelling site where the pottery is found in a very fragmentary state. Judging by the depth of the cultural remains, the average being about $7\frac{1}{2}$ feet and the maximum 12 feet (the depth of the fourth square), the deposit must have been gradually accumulated over a long period of time, not less than several hundreds of years. In the accumulation there are no barren layers ; it is clear that the site was continuously occupied throughout the whole period.

In my opinion this site must be regarded as very rich in content. In the fourth square alone, more than eighteen thousand sherds were unearthed. It must have been densely populated. The area of this site is even larger than Yang-shao. In short, the Hsi-yin Ts'un site is the remains of a big city, the centre of a settled population.

The pottery of Hsi-yin has much in common with that of Yang-shao both in regard to technique and decoration. The most striking parallel is the water-jar with a pointed base. The turn-table was also much used at Hsi-yin. The kiln was quite likely constructed in the same way as that of Yang-shao, because we find the same sort of colouring in the Hsi-yin sherds. The large vessels with open mouths are red both inside and out, while the water-jars with a pointed base are generally red outside but grey inside. The most convenient way of baking a jar with a pointed base is to place it upside down in the kiln. Therefore, the mouth was shut off from the air, and the grey colour was produced inside. The Hsi-yin designs sometimes are based on a peculiar principle, in which the painted area and the blank spaces are made complementary one to the other. We may observe an intentional juxtaposition of red and unpainted ornamental spaces, and black painted designs.

The Hsi-yin pottery has other peculiarities to which no parallels can be found at Yang-shao. Instead of *li* and *ting*, the shapes are simple open pots with straight or bulging sides. The absence of *li* and *ting* is a significant fact when we consider that the three-footed cooking vessel was one of the characteristics of the Red Pottery culture in Honan and the Black Pottery culture in the Great Plain. The shape of the base in the Hsi-yin wares is usually flat and parallel to the rim (Fig. XXXVII, 61–6) not rounded as it is at Yang-shao. A few specimens of a base with a ring-foot (Fig. XXXVII, 67–8) are also found. These bases seem to suggest a more advanced culture than Yang-shao ; but the string-impressed ware at Hsi-yin is inferior in workmanship to either that of Yang-shao or any other site of the same period.

Now let us study the distribution of the sherds in the various strata, particularly with regard to the painted ware. The first column of the following table gives the strata of the fourth square of Hsi-yin Ts'un, the second column the number of plain sherds, and the third the number of painted sherds, and the fourth the percentage of painted sherds. As the totals of the plain and painted sherds are 17,372 and 1,356 respectively, the average is about 7 painted to every 100 plain, or 7 per cent. The fifth column of plus and minus signs represents the proportion of painted sherds in each stratum, showing whether it is higher (+) or lower (−) than the average, or average (o).

In the following table I have adopted Dr. Li's terms in relation

78

to stratification. " Layer A " represents the depth from the surface to 1 metre down (3·28 feet). Layers B to D represent successive depths each of 1 metre.

TABLE 1

DISTRIBUTION OF POTSHERDS IN THE VARIOUS STRATA IN THE FOURTH SQUARE OF HSI-YIN.

Layer and stratum	No. of Plain sherds	No. of Painted sherds	Per cent of Painted sherds	Under (−), above (+) or average (o)
A	272	10	4	—
A 4a	56	2	3	—
b	482	17	3	—
c	127	7	5	—
d	43	4	9	+
e	74	6	8	+
f	258	23	8	+
B 4b	241	11	4	—
c	115	6	5	—
d	175	13	7	o
e	139	8	5	—
f	185	9	4	—
g	146	12	8	+
h	140	8	5	—
i	528	26	4	—
j	2,142	62	3	—
k	428	27	6	—
C 4a	888	90	10	+
b	1,234	117	9	+
c	1,192	162	13	+
d	1,503	130	8	+
e	928	102	10	+
f	526	58	11	+
g	588	56	9	+
h	456	40	8	+
i	663	41	6	—
D 4a	605	34	5	—
b	804	65	8	+
c	1,119	80	7	o
d	784	43	5	—
e	557	31	5	—
f	329	27	8	+
g	189	13	6	—
E 4a	456	16	3	—
Total	17,372	1,356		

N.B.—This table is constructed from Liang's Tables 2 and 3 (Bibl. 18, pp. 32–5).

From the above table we may see that the painted ware has its greatest development from stratum C 4h (depth 2·88 m.) to C 4a (depth 2·06 m.), and the plain ware from stratum D 4*c* (depth 3·25 m.) to B 4*j* (depth 1·6 m.). It is evident that the strata in layer C are the remains of the most prosperous period of this site, as nearly half the sherds were found in this layer (49·3 per cent). Below this layer, there are the layers D and E; the latter has only a very thin stratum which may be included in layer D for the purpose of this survey. In this layer D, we find pottery amounting to about half that of layer C (25 per cent). In layer B, pottery amounts to less than one-third of that of layer C (15·8 per cent). From the third stratum in layer B, pottery finds become suddenly less, and the percentage of painted ware is often lower than the average. The top layer A contains even less pottery (9·9 per cent) than layer B. (These percentages are quoted from Bibl. 18, p. 41, Table 6).

Therefore, I propose to take these four layers as four periods: Hsi-yin I (layer D), Hsi-yin II (layer C), Hsi-yin III (layer B), and Hsi-yin IV (layer A).

CHING TS'UN

Section 52.—The Ching Ts'un site is situated in Wan-ch'üan Hsien in Shansi. It was excavated in 1931 by a joint expedition of the Freer Gallery of Washington and the Normal College of Pei-p'ing. The excavation lasted only six weeks and the area explored was only about 3 acres.

Up to the present, no full account has appeared, and the interim report (Bibl. 27) is written in such a way that it can hardly be used as a basis for a thorough and systematic study. Fortunately, I have seen some of the pottery finds, therefore I can give a preliminary description of them, and supplement the information made in the report.

Section 53.—The pottery finds from Ching Ts'un may be classified and described as follows :—

A. Plain Ware,	B. Decorated Ware.
1. Rough,	
2. Fine.	

A 1. Plain Rough Ware.

(a) Colour.—The common colour is brick-red, but black is also found.

(b) Shape.—The shapes of this ware show much variation. The *li* (Fig. XXXIX, 1), *ting*, and *yen* are the shapes of cooking vessels, while containers, such as water-jars, are commonly found (Fig. XXXIX, *j*, *k*). Some of the jars are nearly 3 feet high and their capacity must have been very large.

(c) Material.—There are two kinds of clay : pure clay and gritty clay ; the latter may be further divided into several kinds according to the proportion of sand mixed with it.

(d) Thickness.—In this respect, the ware is very much like the Hsi-yin coarse ware, i.e. the average thickness about 12 mm.

(e) Method of making.—Moulding and beating were the common methods for making the large vessels. From the marks on the surface of the vessels, we can see that the coiling method was also practised. The small vessels might have been modelled by hand from a lump of clay. There is no indication of the use of the wheel, but the turn-table was certainly employed.

(f) Surface treatment.—The string-impressions are very clear but shallow on the surface. By their arrangement they may be divided into two classes : vertical lines, and groups of slanting lines, the former being the signs of the mould and the latter those of the beater.

A 2. Plain Fine Ware.

(a) Colour.—The colour is usually brick-red, with some variations in tone.

(b) Shape.—Bowls, basins, and jars are the common shapes (Fig. XXXIX, *a–i*).

(c) Material.—Pure clay is the common material, but sometimes gritty clay is used.

(d) Thickness.—The wall is uniformly even, and the variation in thickness is the same as in the Hsi-yin ware.

(e) Method of making.—The coiling, moulding, and beating

81   G

methods were all used. The coiling method was perhaps used for making small vessels only. The turn-table was used in all the three processes.

(*f*) Surface treatment.—The surface is smoothed and polished. Sometimes a red or orange-coloured slip was applied before polishing.

B.   Decorated Ware.

The techniques of this ware are the same as those of the plain fine ware just described. Therefore, we shall describe decoration only.

At this site was found a strange design which was pricked with some kind of a needle on the surface while the ware was still wet. There are also a few very simple incised designs which were either made before, or after, firing.

With regard to painted ware, the surface is often first covered with a dark red slip. There are three kinds of pigments, black, white, and dark red, and they are used in the following ways :—

(1) Black alone. This is the most common kind of painted decoration.

(2) The combination of black and white. This is found on a small proportion of the wares.

(3) White alone. This type of decoration is rare.

(4) Dark red. This is very rare.

A careful study of the drawings (Fig. XL) will lead us to recognize the motifs, which are straight lines, parallel lines, triangles, crescents, and round spots. A number of these motifs are put together to make various designs. The designs are arranged on two systems. On small vessels, say bowls, the designs are often arranged in pairs round a central axis (Fig. XL, *a*). On a single vessel there are, as a rule, not more than two pairs of motifs. On large vessels a series of motifs is often arranged in a continuous ring (Fig. XL, *d*).

The ornamental purpose was sometimes carried out by making handles and knobs into fantastic shapes. The bird's head was a favourite pattern, as it was in the Black Pottery period in Shantung.

Section 54.—From the very beginning of the investigation of this site the excavators have accepted it without any reservation as neolithic. But I believe that it represents at least two periods of culture, Ching Ts'un I and Ching Ts'un II ; the earliest wares belong to a period about contemporary with Hsi-yin IV, and the latest to the Chou. Some of the specimens of plain ware that I have seen I believe to be relics of the Chou period.

Section 55.—Summing up the results of the study of this group, I have arranged the periods of the two Shansi sites in the following order :—

(1) Hsi-yin I,
(2) Hsi-yin II,
(3) Hsi-yin III,
(4) Hsi-yin IV and Ching Ts'un I,
(5) Ching Ts'un II.

CHAPTER V

THE SHENSI GROUP

Section 56.—This group is represented by only one site, Tou-chi T'ai, for no other sites in Shensi have yet been explored. It is on a terrace situated in Pao-chi Hsien, a district just north of the Wei River in the west part of the province. The excavation was started in 1933 by the National Research Institute of Pei-p'ing and is still going on under the leadership of Professor Hsü Ping-ch'ang, late member of the Sino-Swedish Expedition to Chinese Turkestan. During my visit to China in 1935, Professor Hsü kindly showed me his finds, and I have compiled the following brief account of them.

Section 57.—The pottery finds from this site may be classified and described as follows :—

    A. Plain Ware,   B. Decorated Ware.
        1. Coarse,
        2. Fine.

A 1. Plain Coarse Ware.

(*a*) Colour.—The colour is grey.

(*b*) Shape.—Water-jars and *li* are the common shapes. The *li* is tall-legged.

(*c*) Material.—The material is coarse.

(*d*) Thickness.—The ware is uneven, and the thickness is about the same as the plain rough ware of Ching Ts'un.

(*e*) and (*f*) Method of making and surface treatment.—The *li* is moulded as we may see from the string-impressions, which are vertical. On large jars the string-impressions are mainly slanting and not vertical. They are not the products of the mould. I think they were made by the beater and pad method.

A 2. Plain Fine Ware.

(*a*) Colour.—The colour is brick red with some variation in tone.

(*b*) Shape.—Basins, bowls are the common shapes. Like Hsi-yin wares, the bases are mostly flat, because they were made on a turntable. I noticed only one miniature water-jar with a pointed base.

(*c*) Material.—The clay is fine and apparently very carefully washed.

(*d*) Thickness.—The wall is just as even as that of the Hsi-yin fine wares and the thickness is about the same.

(*e*) Method of making.—The ware is mainly modelled by hand. I found signs of the turn-table, but none of the wheel.

(*f*) Surface treatment.—The surface was smoothed or sometimes polished with a pebble, the signs of which are clear.

The method of applying red or white wash is not found. On the whole, the surface treatment is not so well done as it is in Shansi.

B. Decorated Ware.

The technique of this ware is the same as that of the plain fine ware. The most common type of decoration is a black band on the rim.

Section 58.—To sum up, there are no *tou* ; but *li* sherds are common, real painted ware is rare, and there is no Black Pottery. The painted ware is simple in decoration, but accomplished in technique. The coarse grey wares form a large proportion of the finds. Among the associated finds, there are only very few stone tools ; shell and bone implements are also rare.

I conclude that the date of this site is probably a little later than the last period of Hsi-yin.

Chapter VI

THE KANSU GROUP

Section 59.—Under this group I am going to discuss Dr. Andersson's pottery discoveries in the western part of the Kansu province. The boundary of that part of the province has been somewhat changed since Dr. Andersson's journey ; the district of Hsi-ning for instance is now under the jurisdiction of the Ch'ing-hai and not of the Kansu province. As such changes have no archæological significance, I shall not divide the sites into two provincial groups, and I shall include all the pottery finds under the same group of Kansu.

In this chapter I have followed the division of the finds into six cultural groups, as suggested by the discoverer, namely Pan-shan, Ma-ch'ang, Ch'i-chia P'ing, Hsin Tien, Sha Ching, and Ssǔ Wa.

The Pan-shan Cemetery

Section 60.—The Pan-shan burial place lies 43½ miles due south of Lan-chou, the capital of Kansu, close to the west bank of the T'ao Ho, a tributary of the Yellow River. Here the T'ao Ho has cut a gorge about 400 yards deep.

The Pan-shan cemetery comprises four or five grave fields each occupying a hill-top in the area, with Pan-shan as the centre of the group. About 1,600 yards to the south-west of Pan-shan there is Wa-kuan Tsui, and about 1,400 yards to the east lies Pien-chia Kou, where the only undisturbed grave was excavated by Dr. Andersson personally; and Wang-chia Kou is about 1,000 yards to the north (Bibl. 24, Preface v–vi).

A few mortuary pots of the Pan-shan type were also found in other places in Kansu, and were included by Mr. N. Palmgren in one group which he called after the central site Pan-shan. But P'ai-tzǔ

86

P'ing down in the T'ao valley just below the Pan-shan area was the only site from which Dr. Andersson himself excavated typical specimens. The provenance of other specimens reported to have been found in Kao-lan and Nien-po (Lo-tu) was not confirmed (Bibl. 24, Preface vi).

The majority of the specimens were bought from the local inhabitants near the Pan-shan cemetery and the information was gathered from them as well. Fortunately most of the urns were bought in that district either by Dr. Andersson or by his assistants ; there is hardly any doubt that the pots reported by the sellers as having come from Wa-kuan Tsui, Pan-shan, Pien-chia Kou, or Wang-chia Kou, were actually found in the vicinity of Pan-shan.

Section 61.—The pottery finds from this site may be classified and described as follows (this description is mainly based on the information in Palmgren's work, Bibl. 24) :—

A. Plain Ware. B. Decorated Ware,
1. Painted,
2. Decorated in relief.

A. Plain Ware.

This ware is extremely rare (Bibl. 24, Pl. XX, Fig. 6). There is no object in discussing this type of ware as the material is too scanty to provide any criteria.

B 1. Painted Ware.

(a) Colour.—The surface of the ware is always of uniform light brown-red colour, though slight differences are liable to occur on individual vessels. It varies from a warm reddish hue to pure brown, or grey with a tinge of brown or red, though grey is rare.

According to Mr. Palmgren, who judges by colour and hardness, the Pan-shan ware was subjected to a temperature of about $900°–1,000°$ C., and in cases of over-firing to about $1,100°–1,200°$ C. (ibid. p. 5). The ware was baked very uniformly. In a single pot, however, the colour on different parts of the surface may vary a great deal :

reddish patches alternate with less red or greyish patches ; reddish spots appear on a darker ground.

The colour of the fracture is in many cases quite homogeneous, but usually three layers may be distinguished : a superficial layer on the exterior of the pot ; a superficial layer on the inside of the pot ; and a core or middle layer between the two surface layers. The surface layers are generally red while the middle layer is grey. Occasionally the contrary is the case, i.e. grey is on the outside and red on the inside. Between these layers and the core there is rarely any distinct line of demarcation, and this is specially true with regard to the exterior surface layer. The demarcation of the interior surface layer is more conspicuous. " This shows," according to Mr. Palmgren, " that the interior surface has been subjected to more equable conditions of heat and air than the exterior " (Bibl. 24, p. 6). This is quite a sensible explanation, as the air inside the vessel was closed in a limited space, and the air there remained constant, while the air surrounding the outside of the vessel was circulating and changing.

(b) Shape.—In studying the shape of any ceramic group from a cemetery, one is liable to get the mistaken impression that the shapes of urns from graves are more varied than those of the household, because there are more complete vessels to be found in a cemetery than in a dwelling-site, where the pottery finds are as a rule very fragmentary. There is no question that the Pan-shan pottery is remarkable for its variation of forms and sizes. But suppose these vessels were to be broken into small fragments such as those found in Western Honan, one would be led to the conclusion that the shapes of Pan-shan pottery are rather simple.

This assertion needs a few words of explanation. The shape of a vessel is essentially determined by two factors : the form of the three main parts, top, belly, and base, and the relative position of these parts. Among the fragmentary sherds from a dwelling-site, one can only surmise the possible shape by examining the forms of the parts, because the second criterion, relative position, is absent. In this case of Pan-shan, the forms of the belly and the base are very simple, globular and

88

flat respectively, which cannot help much in revealing the shapes of the entire pots. The only part that can be trusted for this purpose is the top of the vessel which includes the neck and the rim. The shapes of the tops produced by the variations of neck and rim are about ten. If we take these ten forms to gauge the possible shapes of this group, as we might be forced to do in dealing with the finds from a dwelling-site, we might be induced to think there are only about ten shapes. Yet, there are actually no less than twenty according to my classification (Fig. XLI), and no less than forty according to Palmgren's (Bibl. 24, pp. 13, 22, 31).

After examining the Pan-shan shapes carefully, we shall find that they have the following typical features : (1) The spherical shape, (Fig. XLI, 14–18), i.e. the tendency to enlarge the capacity of the vessel. (2) Flat circular base. (3) The long-necked vessels usually have two handles on the belly, while the vessels without necks either have no handles at all, or one or two handles near the rim (Fig. XLI, 7, 8, 24). (4) Vessels with suspension holes are always small (Fig. XLI, 3, 4). (5) Ears occur in different types of vessels (Fig. XLI, 17, 22). An ear consists of a semicircular disk with a hole in the middle and a scalloped edge. It is often placed with its diameter in a vertical position, though in a few cases it is horizontal.

(c) Material.—With a few exceptions, the clay has a very fine and uniform quality, with coarser grains removed by washing. In the fracture no sand is visible to the naked eye. Generally speaking, the Pan-shan ware is of a hard and firm quality and not porous.

(d) Thickness.—The ware is uniform with a thickness varying from 3 to 10 mm.

(e) Method of making.—In the necks of some vessels distinct concentric striation is visible on both the inside and the outside. As such signs only appear on the neck, they are by no means indications of the wheel having been used in making the whole vessel. Mr. N. Palmgren advances a theory to explain the occurrence of this striation. He believes that the necks were made with the aid of a " templet ", which, so far as I understand from his description, is a ring-like instrument of wood or similar material, the surface of which was uneven and had imprinted its striations on the moulded clay (Bibl. 24, p. 3). He has not explained the structure of the templet or the method of its employment. To me, this theory is not very convincing, because it cannot explain the following points :—

(1) As the striation is conspicuous on both the inside and the outside, especially of the low-necked pots, it is difficult to imagine how the templet was used. The templet could only have left marks on one side of the surface, but not on both, unless a pair of templets was employed. If templets were used at all, there is no need to use a pair, as a single templet is enough for the purpose of modelling the neck.

(2) The diameter of the mouths of the necked pots of Pan-shan is far from being uniform. It varies from about 4 to 20 cm., with about thirty variations between these extremes. Only very rarely two pots may have the same sized neck. If templets were ever used, the potter should have in hand numerous templets of various sizes. These templets could only be accurately made on a lathe ; but it is unlikely that the lathe was in existence at that time.

(3) If the neck of the vessel was fashioned with the aid of templets, it is difficult to understand why the striation often covers only the upper half of the neck, and especially of the high-necked vessels. (Mr. Palmgren gives in his own work an example, K 5616, Pl. XVII, 3, in which the striation covers the entire neck, but that neck is only about 2 cm. in height.) There is no reason why only the top part of the neck should be made with the aid of the templet.

(4) According to Mr. Palmgren, " On a number of pots there is visible on the inside a couple of centimetres below the edge, a very distinct horizontal furrow, which represents the inner and lower end of the templet. This horizontal furrow is still more clearly seen in the more highly developed types of vessel, the necks of which are more curved at the top (e.g. in the vessel, K 5169) " (Bibl. 24, p. 4). It is difficult to see how such a horizontal furrow could represent the inner and lower end of the templet. As the furrow appears on the inside of the neck, the supposed templet would have been used on the

inside of the neck. Therefore the furrow should represent the outer, not the inner, surface of the lower end of the templet.

If Mr. Palmgren is correct in his supposition about the templets, it means that the templets were only about one or two centimetres in height with sharply cut lower ends. It does not seem to be possible that the potter could make a neck by pressing clay on to the templet without producing an abrupt change of thickness in the wall at a point where the action of the templet ceases. Such a change would, of course, only be visible on the inside of the neck. We should, therefore, not expect a furrow, but a step. As there is but a fine and hardly visible furrow, which is more clearly shown on necks with a pronounced curve, I should think that the Pan-shan necks were certainly not made by means of templets, or anything of the kind.

In short, I cannot accept the templet theory as an explanation of the striation. I take this striation as a sign of the neck having been finished on a turn-table. The reader is requested to refer to the Honan group for the details of this process (Section 13, p. 29). This instrument explains the appearance of signs both inside and outside, the variation in diameter of the striations and their limitation to the rim or top part of the neck, and also the occurrence of the horizontal furrow which was the mark of the tip of the finger. When the neck was made more curved the finger tip could cut a clearer mark on the inside of the neck.

I agree with Mr. Palmgren that the majority of the Pan-shan vessels were built up of rings of clay, which were then smeared over with the same material. The clay was shaped into broad flat bands which were built up in coils until the desired size and shape of a vessel had been acquired. But Mr. Palmgren has failed to mention one important instrument which, I believe, must have been used on the outside of the vessel in the process of smoothing. He only states that the inner surface was smoothed by means of the fingers or with an instrument in the following way :—

" The fingers of the right hand were pressed firmly against the clay, the hand moving from the bottom upwards, while the left hand

91

rotated the jar in a clockwise direction. . . . In this process the cracks between the bands were smeared over by the hand, and the bands were thus baked together as one piece. The spaces between the fingers are clearly visible owing to the more or less high ridges left on the inner walls of the vessels. . . . Thus the inside often exhibits two systems of ridges : (1) Indistinct broad ridges, running in a horizontal direction . . ., which represent the marks made by the bands. (2) Narrower ridges ending indistinctly at top and bottom, but otherwise well-defined, running anti-clockwise obliquely from the bottom upwards, particularly towards the bottom, sometimes radially from the bottom upwards, particularly towards the top. . . . Both systems of ridges may thus be accounted for as indicating the use of the ring-method in the manufacture of these vessels " (Bibl. 24, p. 2).

It is quite right to conclude that this treatment of the inner surface was intended to join the bands together. It must have been done when the clay was still wet, as the fingers have left clear marks thereon. But the point is this : when the clay is wet, the smoothing process could never be done in the way described by Mr. Palmgren without destroying the shape of the pot. Therefore, it is absolutely necessary to use an instrument to help in this process. It might have been a thin shield of some flexible yet firm material. This flexibility enables the potter to produce the desired curve. It was perhaps leather, which could be held on to the outer surface with the left hand, while the fingers of the right hand were pressing on the inner surface. Because the smoothing marks are anti-clockwise, I am inclined to think that the thin shield was used and that the whole operation was done on the turntable. As the smoothing was done with the right hand, the marks produced would naturally be anti-clockwise.

The globular shape and the extraordinary evenness in thickness all may be interpreted as results of this process.

(f) Surface treatment.—After smoothing with the hand or a spatula, the outer surface has undergone a further polishing process. The upper part, covering about two-thirds of the vessel, was intended for the designs ; it was always better finished than the remaining lower part of the vessel which was left plain. But the unpainted part, though not so well tooled as the painted part, is still much smoother than the inner surface.

The polishing was done when the pot was nearly dry, with special implements the surface of which was smooth and hard, like a pebble or a large tooth. A string of smooth seeds could also be used for this purpose.

In a few instances the surfaces of vessels are covered with a thin even layer of clay of finer quality than the body of the ware itself. The method of putting on this coating, according to Mr. Palmgren, was to dip the entire vessel into a thin clay sludge, so that both the inner and outer surfaces of the vessel became covered (Bibl. 24, p. 5).

(g) Decoration.—The decoration was executed by painting black and red upon a light brick-red background. There are many tones of red : brown, yellow, orange, scarlet, purple, violet, and blue. These variations were perhaps due to differences in the quality of the clay, in the thickness and quality of the pigment, and in the duration of firing in the kiln. The quality of the red pigment is sometimes so poor that the contrast between black and red is hardly discernible. The black colour is generally a deep black but it also shows variations of quality. It is often tinged with grey, brown, or red.

The motifs of the Pan-shan pottery are comparatively few in number, and are arranged according to a very simple system. Only a few rare examples of variation from one main style have been found (Fig. XLIII, 51).

The decoration mostly appears on the upper part, equal to about two-thirds of the surface. The base and the lower part, equal to about one-third of the whole surface, remain plain. In the shallow vessels, such as dishes and bowls, the inner surface is painted and not the outer. In a number of mugs and vases, the painted area is much larger, extending right down to the base ; or sometimes only a narrow band above the base is left plain. The painted part between the base and the neck is called by Mr. Palmgren the " mantle ". The lower border of the mantle is marked by a single horizontal, black band, or a combination of two or three decorative elements, also in black. These elements are commonly straight, or wavy bands (Fig. XLIII) and, in a few cases, spiral bands (Fig. XLIII, 4). The upper border of the mantle is at the same time the lower boundary of the decoration of the neck, which is generally much simpler. With a few exceptions, this border-line is red.

The high neck is always decorated (Fig. XLIII, 3, 9, 16–18, 21–4, 29–31, 40, 41, 44, 45, 47, 48), but the low neck may be plain (Fig. XLIII, 2, 10, 12, 14, 19, 28, 32, 33, 42). On the insides of low necks and occasionally of high necks also, decoration may be found. In this thesis we are going to discuss only the decoration of the mantle which is undoubtedly the most important portion of the decorated area. All the designs that appear on the neck can be found on the mantle.

The method of painting seems to have followed a definite procedure : black was put on first, then red. The lower and upper straight boundary lines are sometimes so neatly and exactly executed that I have not the least doubt that they were done on the turn-table. After the pot was dry, it was put on the turn-table, which was rotated by one hand while the other held a brush charged with black fluid against the surface. By a single spin of the table the band could be drawn. After all the black designs were finished, the blanks were filled in with red. This method saves the artisan from handling two kinds of pigments at the same time, and thus prevents the colours from being mixed up. The red was put on as a sort of complement to the black ; it could not be used as the main colour, because its light tone would sometimes be hardly distinguishable from the background. Furthermore it is evident that the potters of that time had not so great a knowledge of the red pigments as they had of the black.

As regards construction, the Pan-shan designs may be classified into the following groups : (1) The main motifs in complicated forms, occupying a conspicuous or central part of the vessel. These motifs are, as a rule, executed in black. (2) Auxiliary motifs. These motifs are used to fill in the spaces between the main motifs, and they are usually executed in red. (3) The boundary motifs. These are used to divide one decorated zone from the other, and also one design from the other in the same zone.

As it appears to me, the main motifs of the Pan-shan group were executed in a very unusual way. They are by no means entirely drawn free-hand, as it has been taken for granted that they were. I think a certain number of mechanical aids were used. The mechanical character of the Pan-shan designs can easily be recognized by comparing them with free-hand work. The most obvious design of a mechanical nature is the so-called " death pattern ", which I prefer to call " tooth pattern ". Dr. Andersson describes the construction of this pattern in the following words : " From two black fields saw teeth project towards each other, but between the saw teeth there is a red or violet band which is just touched by the tips of the saw teeth " (Bibl. 5, p. 315). The main features of this pattern appear best from Fig. XLIII, 2, 32–4, 36, 45–6. I have reproduced this pattern with the aid of a stencil which I cut out of paper. It consisted of a narrow strip of paper with tooth-like indentations along one edge. Some such stencil must have been used in ancient times, and the material of which it was made was probably leather or some other flexible substance.

Of course, I do not mean to say that all the main designs on the Pan-shan pots were done by mechanical aids, but most of them were. A few designs are obviously free-hand imitations of mechanical work.

As the painting was done on a turn-table, the lower half of the pot was in rather an inconvenient position for painting. That is one reason why it was plain. Vertical lines are rare and they appear to be very poorly drawn. On the contrary, horizontal lines are correctly drawn and neatly finished ; that is because they were drawn with the aid of the turn-table, while the vertical lines were drawn by hand.

In the classification of the motifs, I have adopted Mr. N. Palmgren's scheme of dividing all the Pan-shan designs into nineteen families. But I have not subdivided each family into early, middle, and late styles, because I think such an arbitrary division, without the evidence of stratification, of the finds from the same cemetery, or probably the same tomb, is hardly justifiable. The numbers given below refer to my own illustrations.

Family 1.—Horizontal bands. Fig. XLIII, 1–5.

Family 2.—Zigzag bands. Fig. XLIII, 6–7.

Family 3.—Semicircles. Fig. XLIII, 8–9.

Family 4.—Garlands. Fig. XLIII, 10–12.

Family 5.—Patterns resembling primitive ladders. Fig. XLIII, 13.

Family 6.—Scattered circles. Fig. XLIII, 14.

Family 7.—A horizontal row of small circles. Fig. XLIII, 15–16.

Family 8.—Five large circles. Fig. XLIII, 17–18.

Family 9.—Lancet-shaped or shield-like pattern. Fig. XLIII, 19–20.

Family 10.—Square or check pattern. Fig. XLIII, 21–7.

Family 11.—Spirals. Fig. XLIII, 28–31.

Family 12.—Bands running obliquely from the top downward. Fig. XLIII, 32–4.

Family 13.—Complicated arcs or garlands. Fig. XLIII, 35–6.

Family 14.—Horizontal rows of lancet-like leaves in ground colour. Fig. XLIII, 37–8.

Family 15.—Black spool or vase-shaped surfaces with a central band alternating on the mantle with narrow beaker-shaped surfaces filled with close-meshed trellis-work. Fig. XLIII, 39–41.

Family 16.—Bottle-like pattern, filled with a trellis pattern. Fig. XLIII, 42–4.

Family 17.—Vertical bands and trapeziform fields. Fig. XLIII, 45–6.

Family 18.—Broad, black horizontal bands with partly painted circular designs. Fig. XLIII, 47–8.

Family 19.—Horizontal narrow bands and lines. (Called Rope pattern by Palmgren.) Fig. XLIII, 49–50.

Rare pattern.—Fig. XLIII, 51.

B 2. Ware Decorated in Relief.

In contrast to the richly painted ware from the same area, we shall have to deal with a totally different kind of ware with ornamentation, which consists of applying bands of the same sort of clay on to the vessel in decorative designs which stand out from the surface. A modern parallel to this technique is the so-called " sprigged ware ". Sometimes the decoration was incised, but the incised ware is rare. I shall not include it in this thesis as the material is too scanty.

Among the collection from Pan-shan, this ware (B 2) forms only a small minority. But in those graves excavated by Dr. Andersson, some pots of this kind were found in greater numbers (Bibl. 24, p. 36).

(*a*) Colour.—This ware is usually grey, or occasionally greyish red or grey with red patches. It is not so well fired as the painted ware. The average temperature reached is about 800° C., according to Mr. Palmgren (ibid., p. 38).

(*b*) Shape (Fig. XLII).—From the six shapes shown in the drawings it is evident that we have here a unique group, simpler in appearance than the painted ware. The sizes are always small. The largest of them is as big as the medium-sized painted vessels.

This ware shares some of the features of the painted vessels, such as the large handles, the globular body, and flat base. But the neck is less pronounced ; sometimes there is no neck at all.

(*c*) Material.—This ware was made of a special kind of clay which contains a strong admixture of sand and other ingredients. On the surface, grains of quartz, felspar and mica are clearly visible, and grains of lime are often found in the fracture. These foreign materials make the pots look rough and uneven.

(*d*) Thickness.—Taking the neck as the standard, the average thickness is about 4 to 6 mm.

(*e*) and (*f*) Method of making and surface treatment.—The method of making is the same as that of the painted ware, i.e. ring-building. On the underside of the base impressions of matting are sometimes visible. Such impressions were not made to serve as an ornament, because the bottom of a vessel, like the sole of a shoe, is not the proper place to carry ornaments. As Mr. Palmgren has rightly remarked, the ornaments of the Pan-shan pots were intended to be seen from above (Bibl. 24, p. 3). We cannot say that these impressions were those of matting on which the pot was placed while in the process of building, because in this ware the wall was made first, and the bottom slab was the last step in the process of making the body. Moreover, there is no doubt that this ware was made by ring-building in which matting does not play any part. The only other possible explanation is that the impressions were made simply for the purpose of roughening the surface. In this ware it was the custom to make the whole surface rough and not to polish it in any way. The rough surface may be produced by means of modelled relief, incising, or impressing with a mat or some other kind of rough material ; we find all these three methods used in this group, though the incising method is comparatively rare.

The object of a rough surface may be briefly explained. In the case of the cooking vessel, a rough surface is always preferable to a smooth surface, because the surface area is larger and can absorb more heat, and also because it prevents cracking on exposure to heat or to a sudden change from heat to cold. Only when the sand is very fine and uniformly blended with clay, as it is in some of the cooking pots of the Black Pottery period, the surface may be fairly smooth.

(g) Decoration.—The decoration of this ware is mainly carried out with clay strips arranged in simple patterns in relief. Moist clay strips were affixed to the surface of the vessel by pressure with some implement like a slender stick of bone or wood, the marks of which may be seen on the surface of the strips.

The decoration of this ware appears mostly on the upper part of the vessel. But it is also common for the lower part of the vessel to be ornamented with one or two horizontal bands. The motifs are either groups of parallel strips with changing directions, zigzag strips, or semicircles.

Section 62.—This ware was constructed in the same way as the painted ware ; both were found together in the same graves and are contemporaneous. The function of the ware with decoration in relief is, however, different from that of the painted ware. These rough pots were cooking vessels. The admixture of sand in the clay, the rough surface, and the darkened appearance, or occasional occurrence of soot on the surface, all testify to such a function.

This ware was burnt at a lower temperature (800° C.) than the painted ware, which was fired to a temperature of between 900°–1,000° C. The colour of this ware is mainly grey, showing evidence of a reducing condition of firing. We may suppose that this ware was burnt in a kiln which was in some respects different from that used in burning the red painted ware.

The size is comparatively much smaller than that of the painted pots. This is nothing strange. In prehistoric China very small cooking vessels were generally used. As a matter of fact, the diameter of the body of this ware varies from 50–140 mm., and is about the same as that commonly found among the cooking vessels of the Black Pottery period.

As the surface of a cooking vessel was liable to be blackened by fire, the ornamentation of it by painting had no purpose. If it was to be ornamented at all, it could only be done by an alteration of the surface itself, i.e. by making the design on different levels from the surface of the vessel either by incising, impressing, or modelling in relief.

In this type of ware the application of clay strips served another purpose besides ornamentation. It also made the wall of the pot strong and prevented cracking. (This contrivance was sometimes used during the Shang-Yin period.) That is why we find sometimes that strips were laid on the surface rather carelessly, apparently without regard for ornamentation (Bibl. 24, Pl. XXI, Fig. 11), and that is also why horizontal bands often appear near the widest portion of the body where cracking was more likely to occur.

The technique of modelled relief was entirely different from that of painting. Instead of using brush and paint and working on a smooth surface, clay strips and pointed sticks were employed to execute designs

99

on a rough surface. There are no traces of any comb-like instrument, die, or string having been used for making impressions.

The relative date of the Pan-shan pottery will be discussed later.

THE MA-CH'ANG SITES

Section 63.—By the term " Ma-ch'ang ware " all the pottery finds from more than fifteen sites are included. These places are distributed in a region corresponding roughly to the districts of Yü-chung, Kao-lan, T'ao-sha, Lin-t'ao (formerly Ti-tao), and Lo-tu (formerly Nien-po). The typical specimens are found in some graves at Ma-ch'ang Yen in Lo-tu Hsien.

Section 64.—The pottery from this group of sites may be described as follows (this description is mainly based on the information in Palmgren's work, Bibl. 24) :—

(*a*) Colour.—The Ma-ch'ang ware is paler and has a greyer tone than the Pan-shan ware. The ware was also fired in the kiln in piles one on top of the other. Owing to the pots being in such close contact, small areas of painted designs may become blurred or obliterated.

(*b*) Shape.—The variation of shape is no less marked than in the Pan-shan group. We can see from the drawings (Fig. XLIV), that the common shapes copy those of the Pan-shan period. Nevertheless, there are some differences. The tall pots (Fig. XLIV, *h, i, j,*) are more slender than the same forms of the Pan-shan group. The necks tend to be lower, and mouths smaller. The ears, such as those on the high Pan-shan necks, are absent. There are only a few peculiar shapes which are not found in the Pan-shan group at all, such as the *min* (Fig. XLIV, *c*), and certain jars (Fig. XLIV, *w*).

(*c*) Material.—The material of the Ma-ch'ang ware is slightly inferior to that of the Pan-shan ware. The Ma-ch'ang ware has, as its chief characteristic, a small-grained texture due to the admixture of fine sand in the clay. Sometimes lime is also found in it.

(*d*) Thickness.—The thickness varies between 3 and 8 mm., with an average of about 5 mm.

(*e*) Method of making.—Like the Pan-shan ware, the Ma-ch'ang pots were built up of rings, which were smeared over with clay so as to cover the joints. But the traces of this constructional process are not so easily discerned as in the Pan-shan ware. Besides ring-building, the method of direct modelling by hand was possibly applied to the construction of small vessels. There is no trace of the wheel, and the concentric striation on the necks is due to trimming on the turn-table as I have explained in connection with the Pan-shan wares (Section 61, pp. 89–91). The impressions of woollen mats on the exterior of the base of vessels are the same as those found on pots with relief decoration in the Pan-shan group (Section 61, pp. 97–8).

(*f*) Surface treatment.—The outer surface was sometimes so thoroughly worked that except in extremely rare cases the traces of rings cannot be discerned. The upper part of the vessel was more carefully treated than the lower part and the base was also made very smooth. As a general rule, the outer surface was coated with a thin layer of clay which is of finer quality than the ware itself. One specimen was found (Bibl. 24, p. 90) on which the slip had been applied on to the surface with a brush about 2 cm. broad, which proves that the brush was used by the potter at least as early as the Ma-ch'ang period.

In contrast to the exterior surfaces of the Pan-shan ware, which is well smoothed and polished, the majority of the Ma-ch'ang pottery appears dull, and is pitted with tiny holes. Very often the surface was deliberately scratched with some hard substance. Finger-marks are also discernible on the scratched surface.

(*g*) Decoration (Fig. XLV).—What I have said about the methods of execution, and the arrangement of the painted designs in connection with the Pan-shan ware (Section 61, pp. 93–5) is also applicable to this ware. As regards the motifs, I have also adopted Mr. N. Palmgren's scheme of classification, but I have not subdivided each family into three styles, early, middle, and late. The numbers in parentheses given below refer to my own illustrations.

Family 1. Four large circles (Fig. XLV, 1–7).

Sub-family 1 (Fig. XLV, 1–2).

Sub-family 2 (Fig. XLV, 3).
Sub-family 3 (Fig. XLV, 4).
Sub-family 4 (Fig. XLV, 5).
Sub-family 5 (Fig. XLV, 6).
Sub-family 6 (Fig. XLV, 7).

Family 2. Anthropomorphic patterns usually alternating with circles (Fig. XLV, 8–11).

Family 3. The cowrie pattern (Fig. XLV, 12–15).

Family 4. Horizontal zigzag bands (Fig. XLV, 16–17).

Family 5. A horizontal row of reduplicated rhomboids (Fig. XLV, 18–20).

Family 6. Squares (Fig. XLV, 21).
Sub-family 1 (Fig. XLV, 22).
Sub-family 2 (Fig. XLV, 23–4).
Sub-family 3 (Fig. XLV, 25).
Sub-family 4 (Fig. XLV, 26).

Family 7. A row of trellis-filled circles (Fig. XLV, 27–9).

Family 8. Band of angles (V-shaped forms) pointing left (Fig. XLV, 30).

Family 9. Lines grouped together into bands forming more or less meander-like complexes (Fig. XLV, 31–2).

Family 10. Horizontal wavy lines with small undulations in ground-colour on a black painted background (Fig. XLV, 33–4). Fig. XLV, 33, has been labelled as Family 9 by Mr. Palmgren, Bibl. 24, Pl. XXVIII, Fig. 7.

Family 11. Narrow vertical lines in a horizontal zone (Fig. XLV, 35).

Family 12. Rhomboids divided into small squares. (Fig. XLV, 36).

Family 13. Horizontal and vertical lines (Fig. XLV, 37).

Family 14. A narrow band with black almond or walnut-shaped dots (Fig. XLV, 38).

Family 15. A horizontal band with an indented meander (Fig. XLV, 39).

Family 16. Swastika-like pattern (Fig. XLV, 40).

Rare patterns (Fig. XLV, 41–50).

Section 65.—Unlike the Pan-shan pottery which mainly comes from a single site, the Ma-ch'ang ware represents a collection from various places distant from each other ; Lo-tu (Nien-po) and Lin-t'ao (Ti-tao) for instance, are more than 100 miles apart.

Judging by the colouring, the Ma-ch'ang ware might have been burned at a lower temperature than that at which the Pan-shan ware was baked. The shapes are mainly similar to those of Pan-shan, though there are a few peculiar shapes found both at Pan-shan (Fig. XLII *q*, *r*, *u*, *v*, and *w*) and at the Ma-ch'ang sites (Fig. XLIV, *c* and *x*). Among the Ma-ch'ang, but not the Pan-shan, shapes there are a few (Fig. XLIV, *c* and *x*) which are similar to the *min* of the Shang-Yin and Chou periods. The material is slightly inferior to that of Pan-shan, but the thickness is more uniform than that of the Pan-shan ware. The method of making is the same sort of ring-building that was used at Pan-shan. Generally speaking, the surface of the Ma-ch'ang ware is less carefully finished than that of Pan-shan. The Ma-ch'ang decoration followed the Pan-shan methods of execution and principles of arrangement ; consequently some of the motifs are alike. (Compare Pan-shan Fig. XLIII, 17, with Ma-ch'ang Fig. XLV, 5 : Pan-shan Fig. XLIII, 6, with Ma-ch'ang Fig. XLV, 17 ; Pan-shan Fig. XLIII, 29–31, with Ma-ch'ang Fig. XLV, 47–8). Nevertheless there are motifs peculiar to Ma-ch'ang such as Fig. XLV, 1, 8–10, 30–46, and 50, as there are motifs peculiar to Pan-shan such as Fig. XLIII, 8–12, 32–4, and 39–44. As regards colour, at Ma-ch'ang red became less common and the black band with tooth-like edge became comparatively rare.

The similarity of techniques and of some of the Ma-ch'ang motifs to those of Pan-shan suggests that there may be some connection between the two wares. I suggest that Ma-ch'ang ware was derived from Pan-shan but represents a later and more advanced type ; many of the motifs are the same but are more skilfully executed, and arranged in a more complicated fashion.

OTHER KANSU SITES

Section 66.—Ch'i-chia P'ing.—The Ch'i-chia P'ing site is situated in Ning-ting Hsien, Kansu, and sites yielding the same type of artifacts are also located in T'ao-sha Hsien in the same province. They are all dwelling-sites, and no burial places have been found.

The pottery finds from these sites may be divided into four categories (Bibl. 3, p. 11, and Bibl. 5, p. 262) as follows :—

(1) Plain coarse ware. It is a grey ware with mould-impressions on the surface resembling those on the pots from Pu-chao Chai in Honan (Fig. XXXI–XXXIII).

(2) Plain fine ware. This ware is greyish yellow. The common shape is the high necked jar with two handles (Fig. XLVII, a). The wall is often thin, and the vases are hand-modelled on a turn-table. The lower part of the surface is covered with mould-impressions. Great skill in pottery-making is evident.

(3) The third group is the decorated ware. Its colour is grey like that of the first group, but the collar and handles and sometimes a large part of the body are decorated with designs in dotted lines, produced by a comb-like instrument (Fig. XLVII, b).

(4) One or two vessels are found with a few painted lines (Bibl. 5, p. 262). On the inner surface of the vessel some simple triangles were sometimes painted in violet-red (Bibl. 3, description of Pl. V).

As there are Pan-shan wares found on the surface of the Ch'i-chia site (Bibl. 5, p. 262 and Bibl. 3, p. 20), we must agree with the discoverer that its date should be earlier than Pan-shan. Here we find some trace of painted ware, but it is clear that it has no close relation with the Pan-shan culture. The possibility is that either the Ch'i-chia culture is much earlier than Pan-shan, or it is an independent culture. The presence of the moulded ware seems to suggest that some influence from Honan had already reached this region during the Ch'i-chia period. On the other hand, the combed ware proved that it is likely to be a culture different from the Chinese, because so far no combed ware has been found either in Honan or Shantung. Considering all the facts I am inclined to think that the Ch'i-chia sites are remains of a local culture which has been influenced by the Chinese.

Section 67.—Hsin Tien.—The Hsin Tien cemetery and a dwelling site about 3 miles to its south are situated in the T'ao-sha district of Kansu. The finds therefrom are identified as the remains of a single stage of culture, which Dr. Andersson calls the Hsin Tien stage.

The pottery is often greyish yellow in colour. The usual shapes are jars with a wide mouth, a high collar and two large handles. The base is rather peculiar. Instead of being flat as one may expect, it is often concave. The average height is about 15 cm., and the average diameter of the belly is also about the same. The ware is porous and coarse, much inferior in quality to the Pan-shan and Ma-ch'ang wares. The pots are made by the coiling method, and the surface has been polished. Nearly all the vessels have on the base, and sometimes over the whole vessel, marks of the beater (Fig. LXV), which have been interpreted as traces of cloth impressions (Bibl. 3, Description of Pl. IV). Such marks on the upper part of the vessel are usually smoothed down before the painted designs are applied. The painted ornament is directly applied on to the smoothed surface without any further preparation. In one instance (Bibl. 3, Pl. IV, 2) a red slip was applied before painting. The decorated zone is on the neck and shoulder of the vessel as it is at Pan-shan and Ma-ch'ang. The painting is done entirely by free hand. Instead of covering the decorated zone fully, the decorative patterns are very simple and cover only part of the surface. The painting is in black only. Horizontal bands and narrow wavy lines and triangles are the common patterns (Fig. XLVI). There are some peculiar motifs on the Hsin Tien vessels as we can see from the drawings : (1) A pair of upturned bands, with or without a uniting line (Fig. XLVI, b, c, d). (2) The continuous angular meander (Fig. XLVI, f). (3) The N-shaped figures (Fig. XLVI, c).

The shape, technique, and decoration of the Hsin Tien ware shows clearly that it had little relationship with the Pan-shan ware. In some respects it is more primitive but in others more advanced than the Pan-shan ware.

There is no difference between the household and the funerary wares as there is at Pan-shan and Ma-ch'ang. I believe that the Hsin Tien people led a more primitive life than those other groups of people, though they lived at a later age.

The beater and pad method is similar to that used later in Honan and Shantung during periods when grey pottery was prominent. Some of the motifs such as the meander (Fig. XLVI, f) are so like those on early Chinese bronzes that I am inclined to think that this pottery has been influenced by Chinese culture.

Section 68.—Sha Ching.—The sites, both dwelling and burial, of the Sha Ching stage were found in the Chên Fan district of Kansu. The representative site, Sha Ching, is situated about 10 miles west of Chên Fan.

The pottery is of a reddish colour. The common shapes are mugs of small size, the average height of which is about 15 cm. The material is coarse, mixed with much sand or mica. The ware was made by the beater and pad method and it was finished on the turn-table. The lower part of the surface is covered with beater marks which are very fine like those on the Chou wares, and the upper part is often smoothed and covered with a red slip. Some few vessels are found covered with beautiful designs, consisting of horizontal lines, triangles, and birds (Fig. XLVIII, a, b). The painting is executed in red only and no black is used.

Copper objects, including a winged arrow-head, and cowries, and turquoise beads have been found at this site. The dwelling places are found to have been surrounded by mud walls, a necessary defensive measure for people living in a plain such as Chên Fan (Bibl. 3, p. 18).

From these finds, two kinds of Chinese influence are evident : (1) The beater and pad method of making pottery, and (2) the Chinese ornaments, cowries, and turquoise beads. Judging by the stage which the painted ware had attained, I call these sites the remains of the last stage of painted ware in Kansu. I am inclined to put this stage after the Hsin Tien stage, because of its advanced technique of pottery-making, and the obvious Chinese influence.

106

Section 69.—Ssŭ Wa.—The Ssŭ Wa cemetery is situated in Lin-t'ao (Ti-tao) Hsien in Kansu. It was found near a dwelling site of the Pan-shan stage.

The urns are plain and large, of a brick-red or reddish colour. The common shapes are jars (Fig. XLIX, c) with what Dr. Andersson calls a saddle-shaped mouth (Bibl. 3, p. 18). There is a hollow-legged vessel, li, also with a saddle-shaped mouth (Fig. XLIX, c). The body of the jars is oval in section, and I believe these pots are so designed as to be easily portable. The two handles are fitted on to the top part of the vessel (Fig. XLIX). Between the two handles there is often an indented ridge which serves as an ornament (Fig. XLIX, b, c). The average height is about 24 cm. The material is very coarse, mixed with a large proportion of sand. The ware is made by hand and the surface is roughly smoothed with the wet hand.

Every characteristic of the pottery seems to testify that the Ssŭ Wa culture is not Chinese, though it might have been influenced by that culture.

The presence of the li suggests that the Ssŭ Wa culture had been influenced by the Chinese at some date after the introduction of this type of vessel into the Plateau area, which, I believe, occurred probably during the period between the end of the Shang-Yin and the early part of the Chou dynasty.

Section 70.—Dr. Andersson has demonstrated by a study of the stratification that Ch'i-chia is earlier than Pan-shan (Bibl. 3, p. 20), and Pan-shan (Yang-shao) is earlier than Hsin Tien (Bibl. 3, p. 22). But it is evident to me that these sites do not represent continuous epochs of one single culture ; on the contrary, the Ch'i-chia and Pan-shan wares are so different from each other that they could not have been evolved in one continuous development. The same striking difference is found between the Pan-shan, or Ma-ch'ang on the one hand, and Hsin Tien wares on the other, and it is clear that they could hardly have been direct relatives. Dr. Andersson has placed the Ssŭ Wa ware in the period after Hsin Tien, but I am unable to accept his view. The Ssŭ Wa ware is similar in one technique to the Pan-shan ware, i.e. the use of decoration in modelled relief, and it shows no influence of the technique of the fine beater, which we know was introduced from Honan at a time corresponding to the Hsin Tien period. I put Ssǔ Wa between Ma-ch'ang and Hsin Tien. But I agree with Dr. Andersson in assigning Ma-ch'ang after Pan-shan and in regarding Sha Ching as the last stage of the Kansu Group, as evidenced not only by pottery but also by associated material. But to my eyes Sha Ching ware is no direct descendant of the Hsin Tien ware, and I believe its date is probably many centuries later.

To sum up, these various sites may be arranged in a chronological order as follows :—

        (1) Ch'i-chia P'ing
        (2) Pan-shan
        (3) Ma-ch'ang
        (4) Ssǔ Wa
        (5) Hsin Tien
        (6) Sha Ching.

CHAPTER VII

THE MANCHURIAN GROUP

Section 71.—This group consists of the pottery finds from three sites, Sha-kuo T'un, Tan-t'o Tzŭ, and Kao-li Chai.

SHA-KUO T'UN CAVE

Section 72.—The following description is based on the information in Dr. Andersson's report on the excavation of this cave, Bibl. 2.

The cave deposit of Sha-kuo T'un was found in a limestone hill in south-western Manchuria about one mile south-east of the railway station of Sha-kuo T'un, which is on the branch line of the Peking Mukden Railway running from Nü-êrh Ho to the coal mines of Nan P'iao.

The size of this cave was about 16–19 feet long, 3–16 feet broad, and 3–9 feet high. It was partially filled with a sediment, mainly of a grey loam, mixed with sand and slabs of limestone.

The pottery was found in a very fragmentary state. It was only possible to reconstruct the forms of two pots.

The contents of the layers of this cave, starting from the bottom, are as follows : the sediment of layer I was whitish grey loam. In comparison with the contents of the other layers, this one was the poorest. Nevertheless, small fragments of charcoal were found in small quantities, and a few potsherds. Among the four pieces of painted sherds in the whole collection of finds, three were from this layer. A double-ring of stone was also found in this layer. No human bones, but fragments of animal bones were unearthed in this layer. Layer II was the richest. Nearly all the artifacts and human bones were found in it. The sediment was much darker in colour, approaching black, owing to the presence of charcoal. Layer III was also of dark colour, nearly black, owing to the presence of charcoal. A number of animal bones were extracted from this layer. Layer IV consisted of grey loam with limestone slabs. A few potsherds, mussel shells, animal bones, and human bones were found, and also a few marble " buttons " (Bibl. 2, p. 17) and two shell rings. Layer V was another distinct stratum of dark colour due to the presence of charcoal. In it were found animal bones and a few human bones. Layer VI consisted of grey loam and limestone slabs with a few artifacts and animal bones. The surface layer (VII) was also a sediment of grey loam. Two coins were found in it, one bearing the inscription *hsiang fu yüan pao* (A.D. 1008–1016 of the Northern Sung dynasty) and the other *ta ting t'ung pao* (A.D. 1101–1189 of the Chin dynasty). They were found at a depth of only about 10 mm. from the surface (Bibl. 2, p. 35).

Section 73.—The pottery finds from this cave may be classified and described as follows :—

A. Plain.	B. Decorated.
1. Coarse,	1. Painted,
2. Fine Red,	2. Incised,
3. Fine Black.	3. Impressed.

A 1. Plain Coarse Ware.

(*a*) Colour.—The common colour is brown with tones varying from yellowish to reddish. A brighter brown colour is also found with different shades of brick-red.

(*b*) Shape.—The bowl is the common shape (Fig. L, *a, b*). Tall jars are also found (Fig. L, *c*).

(*c*) Material.—The material is coarse with a large proportion of sand and particles of rock.

(*d*) Thickness.—The ware is thick-walled and uneven, sometimes as thick as one centimetre or even more (5–12 mm.).

(*e*) Method of making.—This ware is mainly rough hand-work.

(*f*) Surface treatment.—The outer surface bears either mat or string-impressions. The inner surface is also rough but without the impressions of either string or matting.

A 2. Plain Fine Red Ware.

Only a few sherds of this ware were found.

(*a*) Colour.—The colour is light brick-red.

(*b*) Shape.—The shapes are bowls of small, simple, but graceful form.

(*c*) Material.—The material is fine. The ware is soft. A fine powder comes off on handling.

(*d*) Thickness.—The wall is even and thin, about 5–8 mm.

(*e*) Method of making.—One piece shows evidence of being wheel-made. Judging by the shapes of the rim, I think some of the others were probably hand-modelled.

(*f*) Surface treatment.—Smoothing while the pot is still wet is the common process.

A 3. Plain Fine Black Ware.

Only two pieces were found.

(*a*) Colour.—The colour is nearly black or dark brownish-grey.

(*b*) Shape.—One of the shapes is a *tou* (Fig. L, *f*) and the other cannot be distinguished.

(*c*) Material.—The clay is finer than that of the plain coarse ware.

(*d*) Thickness.—The wall is uniformly even, varying in thickness from about 4 to 5 mm.

(*e*) Method of making.—I cannot agree with Dr. Andersson that this ware is hand-modelled because both outside and inside surfaces are highly smoothed and burnished and all constructional marks have thereby been destroyed. Judging by the shape and the burnished surface I think it is wheel-made.

(*f*) Surface treatment.—The surface is burnished to a shiny appearance.

B 1. Painted Ware.

Three pieces were found in Layer I and one badly defaced in Layer II.

(*a*) Colour.—The colour varies from a deep brick-red to reddish grey tones.

(*b*) Shape.—Judging by these few specimens, the vessels were small. One piece represents the shape of a bowl (Fig. L, *d*).

(*c*) Material.—The material is somewhat coarser than that of the plain fine black ware.

(*d*) Thickness.—The ware is thin-walled, about 5 to 8 mm. thick.

(*e*) Method of making.—Signs of the potter's wheel were found on two pieces.

(*f*) Surface treatment.—The surface was smoothed and red slip was applied to it. The inner surface was sometimes rough and furrowed by deep broad grooves.

(*g*) Decoration.—A broad black band is one kind of the painted designs (Fig. L, *d*2, *d*3). Except one specimen, the black paints flaked off very readily.

B 3. Impressed Ware.

The techniques of this ware are the same as those of the plain coarse ware. The designs consist of intersecting lines which were impressed by means of a piece of string.

Section 74.—The discovery of many kinds of pottery in the same cave shows that its inhabitants either had free communication with the outside world, or else had great skill in pottery-making.

There are two kinds of bowl rims, therefore there must have been two kinds of vessels. One is the common hemispherical shape of ancient China, while the other has a thick rim and flat bottom (Fig. L, *a*). The latter has a string-impressed surface which is rarely found on bowls. With regard to the painted ware, we notice the same imperfections as are to be found in the ware of Tan-t'o Tzŭ in S. Manchuria ; the paint is very loosely attached. It has been proved that the Tan-t'o Tzŭ ware was decorated after firing (Bibl. 9, pp. 8–9). But the question with regard to Sha-kuo T'un has not yet been studied. The ring-foot of the Sha-kuo T'un ware (Fig. L, *e*) is also found among the wares of Tan-t'o Tzŭ (Fig. LII, *d*).

Dr. Andersson believes that all these ceramic finds from the cave were local products (Bibl. 2, p. 22). If this is true, the cave dwellers must have mastered the art of making pottery both by hand and by means of the wheel. But I think it is unlikely that the people who lived under such simple conditions as revealed by the contents of the cave could have been so skilled and experienced in the ceramic art.

In my opinion, there are two kinds of cultural remains in this cave, Chinese and native (Manchurian), the latter forming a larger proportion. Coarse wares, especially the incised ware in Layer I and the string-impressed ware in the upper layers, are native products. The red wares, painted and fine, and the black ware represent Chinese cultural products.

As the Chinese products make up only a minor proportion of the whole collection, it is likely that the original inhabitants of this cave were not Chinese, but ancient Manchurians. In the richest layer (II) we find pottery, artifacts, and ornaments most of which are of Manchurian origin. The only class of objects, which is probably not Manchurian, consists of the human bones.

The human bones found in the cave were splintered, broken, and often burnt. They were identified by Dr. D. Black as similar to the present day northern Chinese (Bibl. 7, p. 98). It does not follow that the inhabitants of the cave were Chinese. On the contrary, the fragmentary state of the bones may serve as another evidence for my theory that the inhabitants were not Chinese. Dr. Andersson thinks that the strange state of the human bones is evidence of cannibalism. I agree with him so far, but I think that the Chinese were the victims. The ancient Manchurians might have hunted and captured some Chinese and brought them into the cave where the cannibal family was waiting for a feast. The fragmentary and burnt conditions of the bones suggest that the bones were also used as fuel for the camp fire.

As regards the use of the cave Dr. Andersson suggests three alternatives, a burial place, a dwelling place of cannibals, or a votive site. The first alternative need not be considered in view of the broken and scattered and often calcined state of the human bones. The second alternative has not been either proved or discarded by Dr. Andersson. But he is inclined to think that this cave was a votive site, where religious ceremonies including the sacrifice of human lives were performed (Bibl. 2, p. 38). That means that the cave was often visited but not inhabited by the votaries.

Dr. Andersson suggests that certain artifacts from this cave deposit were objects intended for votive purposes, especially the mussel rings. He asserts that these rings could hardly have served any practical purpose as they were much too fragile to stand any wear and tear (Bibl. 2, p. 39). But we must remember that mussel shells become fragile only after decomposition. When fresh they are quite strong, and even suitable for making tools such as those which we find at Lung-shan (Bibl. 34, pp. 83–5).

The second alternative that it was a dwelling place seems more probable to me for the following reasons: (1) From the fragmentary potsherds of varying quality not a single complete pot can be reconstructed. If a pot were broken as part of some ceremony (similar to that used in funerals in North China at the present day), we should expect to find all the fragments in the cave. (2) There are three black ashy layers (II, III, V) in the deposit. The thickest black layer (II) is also the richest layer. This is a typical feature of a dwelling site. (3) A large proportion of the artifacts in the deposit is apparently intended for practical purposes, for instance we find pots, stone scrapers, borers, arrow-heads, celts, and bone implements.

Dr. Andersson believes that the whole sequence of the first five layers is the remains of one and the same cultural stage which is best represented by the rich finds in Layer II (ibid., p. 37). But I think that the cave deposit may be taken as an indication of seven periods. Layers I, IV, and VI were only temporarily inhabited, while II, III, and V were occupied for longer periods, and the surface layer was formed by natural agencies, for the coins found there show that it was visited by people not earlier than the Sung (A.D. 960–1277).

The lowest layer represents a very late stage of the painted pottery.

Its technique is that of the black or red ware of Lung-shan I. The incised ware is the same as that of Tan-t'o Tzŭ.

Layer II contains a large quantity of string-impressed wares which are evidently much influenced by the Shang-Yin pottery. *Li* of late Chou type were found in this layer and also in the upper layers. The date of this layer cannot be earlier than the Shang-Yin, but it must be earlier than the Kao-li Chai site in Southern Manchuria, because grey pottery with fine beater marks is entirely absent.

Only a few objects were found in Layers III–VI. It is quite evident that human activity in this cave was at its height during the period of Layer II. The types of *tou* and *li* testify that the date of Layers III–VI cannot be earlier than the period of Eastern Chou (722–221 B.C.).

In short, the history of this cave deposit starts from some date in the Black Pottery period and continues to Eastern Chou, without counting the date of the surface layer.

TAN-T'O TZŬ

Section 75.—My description of the pottery from Tan-t'o Tzŭ and Kao-li Chai is based on the information in Professor K. Hamada's publication entitled *P'i-tzu-wo* (Bibl. 9).

Both the Tan-t'o Tzŭ and the Kao-li Chai sites are situated on the north-eastern corner of the Japanese leased territory, Kuantung district, in the Liao-tung peninsula of Southern Manchuria. They are only about 200 feet apart.

The Tan-t'o Tzŭ site is on the top of a rocky mound about 36 feet high composed of granite-complex covered with alluvial soil. Its ground plan is an irregular triangle, the greatest length of which is about 360 feet and the greatest width 180 feet. The top part of the mound is somewhat flat, but the sides are steep. The thickness of the cultural deposit varies from place to place, ranging from a few inches to about 6 feet.

Section 76.—The pottery finds from Tan-t'o Tzŭ may be classified and described as follows :—

A. Plain Ware, B. Decorated Ware (called A 2, ibid.).
  1. Rough (called A 1, ibid.),
  2. Black (called A 3, ibid.).

A 1. Plain Rough Ware.

(*a*) Colour.—The colour of this ware is mainly black, but its tone is far from uniform. Even on the same vessel various tones may occur. The oxidizing conditions of the kiln must have been very poor. The temperature is estimated by Professor K. Hamada to have been some degrees below 1,000° C. (Bibl. 9, p. 6).

(*b*) Shape.—The common shapes are bowls (Fig. LI, *a*, *b*), jars (Fig. LI, *c*, *f*), and *tou* (Fig. LI, *d*, *l*).

(*c*) Material.—The ware is very rough, and grains of sand are clearly visible on the surface.

(*d*) Thickness.—The thickness of the wall varies from 5 to 15 mm. But the base may be very thick, sometimes up to 20 mm. Judging from the fracture, the thickness of the whole vessel tends to increase towards the base. The edge of the rim is generally the thinnest part of the vessel.

(*e*) Method of making.—There is no sign of the potter's wheel. In some vessels there is evidence of the use of the turn-table. The hand played the chief part in the making of this ware.

(*f*) Surface treatment.—Smoothing with the wet hand was the common method of treating the surface. With the exception of the bowls and *tou*, polishing was rarely practised.

A 2. Plain Black Ware.

In the excavation of the north side two graves were found which contained nine pots, one stone axe, and three beads. The pottery is plain but it shows some improvements as to shape and method of making, when compared with the plain rough ware from this site.

(*a*) Colour.—This ware has the same colour as the plain rough ware.

(b) Shape.—The shapes (Fig. LI, g–j) are different to a certain extent both from the plain rough ware and the decorated ware.

(c) Material.—In some pots it is the same as the rough ware. Some are made of finer material.

(d) Thickness.—This ware is thinner and more even than the plain rough ware. Average thickness is about 6–10 mm. The base shares the same quality of thickness with the plain rough ware (A 1).

(e) Method of making.—This ware was made by means of the potter's wheel. Marks of it may be seen not only on the body but also on the neck.

(f) Surface treatment.—The surface was sometimes smoothed with the wet hand, so the marks of the wheel were destroyed.

B. Decorated Ware.

The painted ware forms a very small proportion of the pottery finds. In the whole excavation only two entire vessels and about thirty fragments were unearthed.

We call it " painted pottery ", but it is to be remembered that it is quite different in one respect from the painted wares from Honan and Kansu. Its painted designs were made after, not before, the vessel was burnt in the kiln. The pigments flake off very easily.

(a) Colour.—The ware is mainly black, or brownish-black, and sometimes brick-red. The designs were painted in white and red, sometimes white and yellow if the ground colour were brick-red.

These three kinds of pigments, white, red, and yellow, have been analysed and identified as ordinary inorganic colours (Bibl. 9, p. 9). They are the pigments usually used for pottery painting. This suggests the idea that the potter had followed the traditional method of applying colours, but avoided burning them in the kiln. The reason for the omission of the burning process is probably this : the kiln of that time was constructed in such a way that it could only produce black and brownish colours, and no bright colours such as red, yellow, or white. If these bright colours had been applied to the pot and fired in the kiln they would have disappeared.

The designs must have been painted by mixing the pigments with some cementing material such as oil, varnish, or other waterproof liquids. After the paints had become dry, they stuck on the surface of the pot. Only through decomposition of the cementing material was it possible for the paints to flake off. If water had been used to mix the pigments the painted designs would not stand weathering or handling.

(*b*) Shape.—The shapes (Fig. LII, *a–d*) are different from those of the plain ware of the same period. They could not have been cooking vessels, because the shapes are unsuitable for that purpose. Quite likely they were containers of dry food or cereals, and some were simply ornaments.

(*c*), (*d*), and (*e*).—The material, the thickness, and the method of making of this ware are the same as those of the plain black ware.

(*f*) Surface treatment.—Though some of its techniques are identical with those of the plain black ware, its appearance is quite different : the surface is well polished, and thickly covered with pigments.

(*g*) Decoration.—The designs (Fig. LII, *a–d*) are much more complicated than those of any other provincial group. As a rule, the designs are executed in two colours on a ware which is either black or brick-red. If the ground colour were black, red and white were preferred, and if the ground colour were brick-red, yellow and white were used.

The relative date of Tan-t'o Tzŭ will be discussed in connection with the Kao-li Chai ware (Section 79).

Kao-li Chai

Section 77.—The Kao-li Chai site is situated about 200 feet west of Tan-t'o Tzŭ on the flat top of the tableland. It covers an area of about 360 feet in length and 20 to 30 feet in width. Its centre is about 45 feet in height, i.e. about 10 feet higher than the Tan-t'o Tzŭ site. All sides are somewhat steep, except the west side which is a slope connecting with the mainland.

Section 78.—The pottery finds from Kao-li Chai may be classified and described as follows :—

A. Plain,

1. Black (called A 3, in Bibl. 9),
2. Black Gritty (called B, ibid.),
3. Grey (called C, ibid).

B. Decorated : incised.

A 1. Plain Black Ware.

This ware is identical with the tomb ware from Tan-t'o Tzŭ (specimens in ibid., Pl. XLIV, 11, 12, 13, and 15).

A 2. Plain Black Gritty Ware.

(a) Colour.—The colour is usually brownish black, sometimes intensified by contact with fire.

(b) Shape.—The common shape (Fig. LIII, e, f) is more or less identical with the steaming vessel, yen, of the Bronze Age. Some shapes are called li in the report, P'i-tzu-wo (Bibl. 9). But so far as I can see, there are no li, though the lower part of a yen may be mistaken for a li. Some are deep pots (Fig. LIII, a, b, c). All these shapes vary much in size.

(c) Material.—The material is very coarse, and the amount of sand is large.

(d) Thickness.—The average is about 10 mm., though the joints and legs may be thicker.

(e) Method of making.—The ware is described as hand-made, but to my eyes the wheel must have been used, as I observed clear signs of the wheel technique. It appears to me, for instance, that the three legs of the yen were made separately on the wheel and then joined on to the body of the vessel.

(f) Surface treatment.—Smoothing by the wet hand is the common method, occasionally polishing was done, though not very successfully on account of the gritty nature of the material.

119

A 3. Plain Grey Ware.

This ware is clearly of a historic period. We may state briefly its main characteristics.

(*a*) Colour.—The colour is generally grey and occasionally red.

(*b*) Shape.—Large basins, *tou* (Fig. LIII, *g*), and jars (Fig. LIII, *d*) are common.

(*c*) Material.—Coarse clay, like that of the late Chou and Han, was used.

(*d*) Thickness.—The thickness is about the same as the black gritty ware, but more even. It varies from about 5 to 12 mm.

(*e*) Method of making.—Wheel technique is used for the most part. In making large vessels, the aid of the beater and pad was required in addition.

(*f*) Surface treatment.—The surface is untouched and often bears the impressions of the beater. Parallel lines cut by the action of the wheel are found. The beater impressions are usually vertical on the top part of the vessel and oblique or horizontal on the lower part.

Decorated Ware : incised.

The cooking vessels are sometimes incised not only on the neck and the body, but also on the base. But the designs are so simple that the purpose of these incisions may be regarded as functional and not ornamental. Other techniques of this ware are the same as those of the rough black ware.

Section 79.—The painted ware of Tan-t'o Tzŭ is fundamentally different from the painted ware of any other group in Honan, Kansu, or even Sha-kuo T'un in Manchuria. The differences are these : the use of two bright colours, red and white, on a dark surface instead of dark colours on a light ground ; and the application of pigments on the vessel after firing instead of before firing.

The black ware of Tan-t'o Tzŭ (A 1), and also the decorated ware (B) show some similarity in shape with the Lung-shan ware in Shantung, for instance the *tou* (Fig. LI, *k*), the painted jar with a peculiarly small

120

base (Fig. LII, *d*), and the tall cooking pots (Fig. LI, *e, f*). Still more striking than these are the similarities between the pots from the graves (Fig. LI, *i, j*), and those of Lung-shan. The wheel technique is used in both groups.

There are two kinds of ware to be found at Kao-li Chai, the native black ware, and the Chinese grey ware. The former is usually made by hand and the latter wheel-made. The incised decoration is rare at Tan-t'o Tzŭ but common at Kao-li Chai. It is a question whether it was developed locally or was introduced from outside.

There was only one piece of bronze found at Tan-t'o Tzŭ while numerous bronze and iron tools of various kinds were found at Kao-li Chai. It is apparent that metal was rarely used by the Tan-t'o Tzŭ people, though that material was not unknown to them. But the Kao-li Chai people used weapons and tools of metal to a large extent, though stone implements inferior in workmanship to those of Tan-t'o Tzŭ were also used.

The connection between these two sites seems to me not to be continuous. The two graves at Tan-t'o Tzŭ which contain the distinctive pottery (type A 2) were perhaps made by the people who lived at Kao-li Chai after the Tan-t'o Tzŭ site was deserted by its former inhabitants.

The Kao-li Chai settlement is dated by the discovery of Chinese coins of the period previous to the first century B.C., i.e. about the time of Western Han. According to Professor Hamada, the date of Tan-t'o Tzŭ is not much earlier than Kao-li Chai, perhaps only by one or two centuries ; also, the people of both sites belonged to one and the same race. Owing to the presence of Chinese artifacts, and objects with distinctively Chinese characteristics, he suggests the idea that these two sites were remains of Chinese colonies which served as trading stations in the journey from Shantung via Korea to Japan. He thinks that the colonization of this area by the Chinese should be dated earlier than the Han dynasty, because he found there an early type of Chinese coinage, such as knife and spade money, and also the *li*-shaped cooking vessel (Bibl. 9, p. 24).

Before expressing my own opinion, let me put together the information I have gathered from the study of the pottery. Professor Hamada has suggested that the pottery of these two sites may be divided into two kinds, local and Chinese. But I think a third division should be made, including pottery made locally but influenced by Chinese products. The real native wares are only the painted and the incised wares (Tan-t'o Tzŭ B, Kao-li Chai B). The real Chinese is the grey ware (Kao-li Chai A 3). The other three kinds of ware (Tan-t'o Tzŭ A 1, A 2, Kao-li Chai A 2) are products due to Chinese influence. Therefore, I am rather inclined to think that there are two cultures which have left their remains on these two sites, the Chinese and the native. The metal tools, coins, and grey pottery are relics of the Chinese. The stone and bone tools and the rough pottery probably belong to the native culture.

During the Tan-t'o Tzŭ period, Chinese influence had already penetrated into this region, though it was not very strong. The sudden occurrence of metal-work in large quantities at the Kao-li Chai site and the rarity of such work at the Tan-t'o Tzŭ site show clearly that the intrusion of Chinese influence was at the beginning gradual but later overwhelming. When the Chinese arrived at Kao-li Chai, the natives were still using stone and bone tools. Thus, according to the two kinds of cultural remains, the Kao-li Chai site may be divided into two periods, Kao-li Chai I and Kao-li Chai II. Judging by coarse wares from Kao-li Chai, I believe the date of its first period is probably contemporary with Sha-kuo T'un III–VI.

Section 80.—Summing up the results of the study of this group of pottery, I have arranged the periods of the three Manchurian sites in the following chronological order :—

    (1) Sha-kuo T'un I and Tan-t'o Tzŭ.
    (2) Sha-kuo T'un II.
    (3) Sha-kuo T'un III–VI and Kao-li Chai I.
    (4) Kao-li Chai II.

PART III

THE POTTERY CHARACTERISTICS

Chapter VIII

TECHNICAL CHARACTERISTICS

Section 81.—This part is devoted to the comparison of the characteristics of the wares in each of the seven provincial groups, and to the explanation of how such characteristics are produced, and also to the study of the changes of these characteristics in the course of time. Taking Honan as the starting point, I shall compare with it the groups which are in the same geographical region and those with which it is proved to have had communication. For instance, N. Honan is compared with W. Honan : Shansi with Honan ; Shensi with Shansi ; Kansu with Shensi, Shansi, and Honan ; Honan with Shantung ; Manchuria with Honan and Shantung.

In the following three chapters the various characteristics of pottery discussed in the Second Part are compared. I have grouped them under three headings as follows :—

Chapter VIII.—Technical characteristics : colour, thickness, material, method of making, and surface treatment.
Chapter IX.—Shape.
Chapter X.—Decoration.

COLOUR

Section 82. N. and W. Honan.—In Northern and Western Honan we can find nearly all the colours of prehistoric wares, the main colours being red, black, and grey. The stratification shows that the red wares in this area are the earliest, black later, and grey the latest. Grey-coloured vessels for cooking purposes are found in small proportion in every stratum.

Shansi, Shensi, and Kansu.—Only a few sherds of Black Pottery have been found in Shansi (Section 97, p. 167), but so far no trace of it has been discovered in Shensi and Kansu, where red and grey are the main colours.

Shantung, Shansi, Manchuria, and Honan.—The rarity of red ware in Shantung is as significant a fact as the rarity of black ware in Shansi. The T'ai-hang mountains form a boundary between the areas in which these two wares are distributed. In Shantung black ware is found in as large quantities as the red ware in Shansi. The colours of the Manchurian wares differ from those of Shantung, but are more or less similar to those of Honan, i.e. the three main colours are found. As regards technique, however, the red and black wares of Manchuria are more akin to the wheel-made wares of Shantung, though of a much inferior quality.

Besides a few rare colours, such as white and brown, the pre-historic wares have only three main colours, red, black, and grey.

RED

The clay of the red ware is fine loess silt which often contains a small percentage of iron compounds (Bibl. 6, p. 9, Bibl. 18, Appendix 2). In the kiln, if the iron can combine freely with oxygen, ferric oxide will be produced which gives a reddish colour ; otherwise, the iron changes into bluish-black ferrous oxides.

The red wares in Honan, Shansi, Shensi, and Kansu are not uniform in colour ; they are brick-red throughout, or brick-red on the surface only ; or one part of the vessel is red and the other grey. The red colour itself may vary in tone.

The frequency of the red-coloured ware does not mean that the red colour was specially favoured during the Red Pottery period. As a matter of fact, white and black colours were more favoured in that period, and that is why the white slip was often applied to the surface and then painted with black.

BLACK

Like the red, the black ware is not uniform in colour ; it is black throughout, or black on the outside and grey inside, or rarely one part of the vessel is black and the other parts are grey. The black colour itself may also have various tones ; the black ware of Shantung is darker than that of Honan.

Black wares may be produced in one of the following three ways :

(1) By special surface treatment the outside surface can be blackened : a hæmatite wash can be applied to the surface and then the ware must be baked in a reducing fire ; or graphite may be rubbed on to the surface after firing ; or the pot may be polished while it is still hot with either resin, varnish, wax, oil, fat, or other similar material.

(2) In a reducing atmosphere the red iron compounds in the clay are reduced to black oxides. Sometimes at the last stage of firing, when the fire begins to die down, some smoke-producing fuel, such as sawdust, is thrown into the kiln which is then immediately closed. Blackening occurs, partly due to the soot and partly due to the reducing action of the carbon present. Or, when the pots are still hot from firing, they are put into a pile with leaves and grass, and thus a layer of soot is deposited on the surface. The soot penetrates deeply into the porous body of the pot (Bibl. 23, pp. 320–6).

(3) By adding some ingredients to the clay, such as manganese oxides, charcoal, or other carbonaceous matter (Bibl. 8, p. 10). The Black Pottery in China is not due to a special surface treatment, because in the typical Lung-shan ware the core is just as black as the surface. Nor can we say it is due to any ingredients in the clay, because in the pseudo-black ware there is a grey or red core underneath the surface. I venture to offer another explanation. As we can see from modern Chinese black wares, the ware produced by a reducing fire is bluish-black when new, and it acquires a black surface through constant use, by being brought into contact with organic matter, such as fat and oil. The carbon produced by the decay of these substances is the main ingredient of the black colour. If the walls are thick as they are in the modern black wares, and the ancient pseudo-black wares, the grease does not penetrate to the core, which remains bluish-black. The typical Lung-shan ware was so thin that the grease was able to penetrate the whole substance.

GREY

As we have mentioned, both the red and black wares are not uniform in colour, but the grey ware differs from them in having more uniform colour throughout. This feature is due to the " imbibing " process (Section 16, pp. 36–7). The period when this process was first used is unknown ; as the uniform grey ware is found to be highly developed in the Shang-Yin period, it must certainly be earlier than the Shang-Yin.

It is mentioned in the *T'ien kung k'ai wu* (Bibl. 26, vol. ii, 4) that a certain temperature must be reached before the ware could get the grey colour by the imbibing process. The purpose is to temper the pots. I think that quite likely the ancient potters got this idea through experience : when a new pot was filled with hot water, sometimes it cracked. In order to prevent this risk, the imbibing process was invented, and the grey colour is the result.

The changes of colour are different in every region. (1) In Shantung, the colour passed through two stages only : black first, then grey. The dates of these two stages have been proved to be later than the Red Pottery period in Northern Honan. (2) In Shansi, Shensi, and Kansu the colour also passed through two stages, red first, then grey ; the former had apparently persisted longer than it did in Honan. (3) In Honan and to a certain extent in Manchuria, the colour passed through three stages, red first, then black, and finally grey. In all these three regions there is a common feature, that is the final grey stage. This is true of all common pottery forms, except the cooking vessels.

THICKNESS

Section 83.—I call a wall thin when it measures 5 mm. and less, I call it medium when it measures 6–9 mm., and thick when it measures 10 mm. and over.

Honan, Shansi, and Shensi.—The red wares in Honan have an average thickness of about 5–6 mm. The minimum is about 3 mm., and the maximum 6 mm. The black wares from Hou-chia Chuang are different from those found at other sites such as Hsiao T'un and Hou Kang. Their average thickness is more than 5 mm., and their variation in thickness is 4–12 mm. Black wares in Honan and Shantung should be divided into two kinds according to thickness. One kind is nearly as thick as the red ware, while the other kind is much thinner. Both these two kinds vary in thickness in the same degree as the red ware. The coarse grey ware from Hsiao T'un in comparison with the coarse ware from Western Honan is really of extraordinary thickness. It is the thickest ware both in Honan and Shantung. Its minimum thickness is 20 mm. and maximum 30 mm.

The red wares from Shansi and Shensi are on the average about 2 mm. thicker than those from Honan, and their variation in thickness is also higher, from 3–13 mm. The coarse wares are thicker than those from Western Honan, but thinner than the grey wares from Hsiao T'un. They vary in thickness to about the same extent as the Hsiao T'un coarse wares.

Kansu, Shansi, and Shensi.—The Kansu pottery specimens as represented by the Pan-shan and Ma-ch'ang red wares are on the average about 3 mm. thinner than those from Shansi and Shensi. The thickness varies from 3–10 mm., i.e. there is less variation than in the red wares from Shansi and Shensi.

Shantung, Honan, and Manchuria.—The black wares in Shantung are on the whole thinner than those in Honan ; their thickness varies from about 1–5 mm. The pseudo-black ware in Shantung has an average thickness of 4 mm., nearly equal to that of the black sherds from Sha-kuo T'un but less than that of the plain fine ware from Tan-t'o Tzŭ. The coarse wares from Shantung have an average thickness of about 5 mm. and vary in thickness to the same degree as the coarse wares from Kao-li Chai (A 1) in Southern Manchuria.

It may be too obvious to mention that the first factor determining the thickness of a vessel is its size. As a rule; large vessels have a thick wall, and small vessels a thin wall. That is because a pot must be strong enough not only to stand by itself, but also to carry some weight, and the strength cannot be derived except from the thickness of the wall.

As I have suggested, the thickness of any ware is closely connected with the method of making. The beater and pad method produced the thickest ware with the most uneven wall. The moulding method produced both thick and medium wares and sometimes, though rarely, thin wares. The throwing method produced thin wares, sometimes medium wares, but rarely thick wares, all of more or less uniform thickness. This is, of course, only true as regards the prehistoric period.

Another determining factor is the material adopted in the making of the ware. Generally speaking, the thin wall is made of fine material, and medium or thick wall of coarse material. The thinnest black ware from Shantung contains the finest material and the thickest Hsiao T'un ware from Honan contains the coarsest material. There are, however, some thick, or medium walled red wares in Western Honan which are made of fine material. In short, the thin ware must be made of fine material, but the fine material may not necessarily be used only for making thin wares.

From the evidence of stratification of the sites in Honan and Shantung, we shall see that the changes in the thickness of the wall took place in certain periods, each change representing the adoption of new techniques. The following table shows the chronological order of the changes. I have only selected the most frequently used wares in each successive period.

(1) Medium, represented by the Red Pottery.

(2) Thin, represented by the Black Pottery.

(3) Thick. This type is represented by the grey wares which are found in nearly every site mentioned in this thesis. It has an origin at least as early as the medium ware, but it only became popular after the thin black ware had declined.

(4) Extra-thick, represented by the Hsiao T'un coarse grey wares.

(5) Uniformly medium, represented by the Chou wares from Hou-chia Chuang III and Lung-shan II.

MATERIAL

Section 84.—Generally speaking, the material of the red wares in the territory extending from Honan to Kansu consists of fine clay carefully prepared, while the material of the black wares in Shantung is as fine or even finer. The similarity of these two wares, red and black, as regards fineness of material is striking, and no doubt is partly due to the fact that the clay is derived from the loess which occurs throughout North China.

The cooking vessels of coarse ware both in the Plateau and in the Plain show great contrast to the contemporaneous containers made of fine ware from the same region. Their material is either naturally or artificially mixed with sand. Later in the full grey pottery period the use of coarse material became general for all types of vessels. The grey wares of the prehistoric period either from Honan, Shansi, Shensi, or Shantung often manifest the same coarseness. In the coarse wares, especially those of the Chou period, fine sand was always chosen and added to the clay in a constant proportion ; but in the earlier wares the particles of sand are larger and less uniform, and the quantity of sand was apparently not limited by any fixed rule.

The intended function of the vessel often determines the material with which it is made. The material of cooking vessels is invariably mixed with sand and originally this may have been accidentally done. At all events, the mixing of sand with the clay makes it less sticky, and it was found by experience to prevent contraction, distortion, and cracking in drying and baking. Also it prevented cracking when vessels were used for cooking. Of course, the processes of refining such as sifting, weathering, washing, and particularly levigating, are also important factors in determining the nature of the clay.

So far as we can see from a study of the strata at the various sites, the material of vessels, except those used for cooking, has undergone obvious changes. But the material of cooking vessels, either in the Red Pottery or Black Pottery period, has remained practically the same throughout the ages. The following are the changes in chronological order which took place in the preparation of material, excluding that of the cooking vessels.

The earliest process is to select or wash the clay to make it fine. Examples of such fine wares are found at Hou Kang I, Hou-chia Chuang I, Yang-shao, Ch'in-wang Chai, Ch'ih-kou Chai, Hsi-yin, Ta-lai Tien I, T'a P'o, Ch'ên Kou, and Liu Chuang. The second process is to levigate the clay in order to make it extra fine. The typical Lung-shan ware is made of this extra fine material, and it is found at Lung-shan I, Liang-ch'êng, Hou Kang II, and Hsiao T'un I. The third process shows a lack of preparation. The material is coarse, containing sand in varying quantities and of varying quality. The representative wares are those from Hsiao T'un II, Hou Kang III, and the coarse wares of Lung-shan I and Kao-li Chai I. The fourth process is deliberately to make the material coarse by the addition of a carefully measured proportion of sand. Wares from Hou-chia Chuang III, Lung-shan II, and Kao-li Chai II, are of material made by this process.

METHOD OF MAKING

Section 85. Northern and Western Honan.—In the method of making, we can see a close similarity between Northern and Western Honan. The popularity of the red-ware bowl with a round base in both regions shows that the hemispherical mould must have been used in the whole of Honan during the Red Pottery period. The presence of cooking vessels with vertical string-impressions in both regions testifies that the belt-mould was a common technique in Honan during the Black Pottery period. In making the large containers, ring-building on a turntable was the usual method. The wheel, as we can see from the recent discovery of Black Pottery both in Northern and Western Honan, was used in the Black Pottery period. The beaten ware, which became common during the Shang-Yin period, had, however, originated in the prehistoric period. Wares bearing beaten designs of squares have been found at Hou Kang, Hsin Ts'un, and Pu-chao Chai, which are all earlier in date than the Shang-Yin.

132

Honan may be regarded as the centre, if not the original home, of the moulded ware. Among the prehistoric sites in Honan, hitherto excavated, nearly all contained specimens of moulded ware. The moulds are of three kinds. The simplest and the earliest form of mould is the hemispherical one. As only bowls are found to have been made by this method, I am inclined to think that it was an ordinary bowl used as a mould for the production of another bowl. Or the mould might have been a thick block of wood, pottery, or stone, with a concave hollow space at the centre to serve as a mould. By experiments I have proved that moulds such as these are quite practicable.

The use of string or textiles is an aid to moulding. It is a method practised both in the Red Pottery and in the Black Pottery periods. The belt-mould, which is likely to have been derived from the string-mould, was used since the early Black Pottery period in Honan when the hemispherical mould was given up. The belt-mould is unsuitable for making the flat base, which consequently has to be shaped by another method, i.e. ring-building, or modelling by hand on matting or basket-work. The beater, as we have said in connection with the Hsiao T'un wares, is simply an improved form of the belt-mould. The difference lies in the fact that the beater in comparison with the mould is much smaller in size, and it can be applied to any part of the vessel in turn.

There are certain characteristics of the moulded ware which may be observed : (1) The moulded pot often has a rounded base, which may sometimes be intentionally flattened in order to make the vessel more stable. In order to get a proper flat base for a moulded pot, its base has to be made separately. A base by this method has sometimes clear mat or cloth-impressions on the outer surface, which have been made in order that they may conform to the surface of the other parts of the vessel. (2) The moulded ware has deep, clear, and always vertical string-impressions on the surface. The high slender *li* most clearly shows these impressions. It was moulded separately in three parts which were cemented together with pieces of the same kind of clay. (3) The moulded ware may also be distinguished by the signs

133

on the inner surface of the vessel ; (*a*) the signs of smoothing with the hand, (*b*) the signs of pressing or scraping with the hand or with an instrument.

The differences between moulding and beating are clear. By the moulding method, the mould is used as the main instrument for producing the vessel, and the pressure is applied on to the inner surface ; while by beating the beater is used to finish the surface and to diminish the thickness of the walls, and the pressure is applied on the outer surface. The marks of the mould are different from those of the beater ; the former are deeper and more regular than those of the latter. On the inner surface of the moulded ware there are clear marks of smoothing or pressing by the hand or by some tool, while on the inner surface of the beaten ware there may be signs of the pad, but seldom the marks of the hand or smoothing tool.

Honan, Shansi, and Shensi.—There are two features shared by Honan, Shansi and Shensi : the moulding method for making the water-jar with a pointed base, and the trimming of rims on the turn-table. In these three provinces the turn-table was sometimes used as a miniature wheel to make small vessels. Such products are more or less similar to wheel work. The main function of such a table is to enable the pot to be easily turned.

Shansi, Shensi, and Kansu.—It seems that the Kansu wares do not resemble the wares from Shansi and Shensi, but were developed independently. From the early to the late cultural periods in Kansu, no trace of the wheel technique has been found. There is some trace of the beater method, and also of the mould. The chief method is to make by hand, especially by ring-building on a turn-table, which is somewhat different from that used in Shansi and Honan. Judging by the size of the vessels and fineness and evenness of their walls it is no exaggeration to say that the Kansu urns represent the best specimens of hand-made ware in the history of ceramic art in China. I have noticed in the rims of the Pan-shan and Ma-ch'ang vases that the bands of parallel striæ are much narrower than those on the pots from Honan, Shansi, or Shensi. That fact leads me to think that the turn-table in Kansu was perhaps more clumsy in construction than that used in Honan, Shansi, and Shensi.

As we can see from the Honan and Shantung finds, small vessels, or miniature pots, are generally made entirely by hand without the aid of any tool or implement. In forming large vessels, like those from Kansu, the clay is modelled on a turn-table by the method of ring-building and the hands are usually aided by some simple tools, such as a shell, a piece of gourd rind, a stick, or a wooden templet. Some peculiar features of this ware may be observed on its surface : it is always smoothed though not necessarily polished, and on the inner surface there are signs of smoothing in a direction at right angles to the horizontal junctions of the clay rings.

Honan and Shantung.—The hemispherical mould and belt-mould of Honan are not found in Shantung. Among the wares of the Red Pottery period in Honan we find the water-jars made by means of the string-mould. In Shantung the string mould is found in the Black Pottery period. During the Chou period in Shantung the beater method became prevalent, but the beater was covered with much finer string than that of the Shang-Yin period. In the Black Pottery period there is no trace of the ring-building method, in place of which we have the wheel technique.

The adoption of the wheel started a revolution in the ceramic industry. The superiority of this new technique over the moulding method was so overwhelming that the old technique had to give way.

The origin of the potter's wheel in China is unknown. From the evidence that I have collected, I should say that the wheel is derived from the turn-table. The turn-table is a wooden disk pivoted on a board fixed in the ground. Only because its size and weight are insufficient, it cannot be used for throwing. If the disk is increased in size and weight, it is possible to work up a momentum sufficient for the potter to apply pressure to the clay without stopping the motion. The simplest form of the wheel, so far as we can surmise from modern survivals, consists of a large single heavy disk of wood, or less frequently of pottery or stone, from 0·3–1·0 m. in diameter, supported a few centimetres above the ground on a pivot.

The advanced stage of the wheel is known as the double-wheel. As used in China to-day it is a mechanism of two wheels, one for propulsion and one for modelling, and each of them is smaller and lighter than that made for the single wheel. As far as the actual products are concerned, it is extremely difficult to tell whether they have been made on a single or double wheel.

The wheel was not used at Hou-chia Chuang II, but it was used at Hou Kang II. So we see that the wheel was started after Hou-chia Chuang II and before Hou Kang II in that part of Honan, and, therefore, its relative date can be more or less ascertained. As it seems to have come suddenly, it may not be a local invention, but an importation, perhaps from Shantung, where the wheel-technique is found to be more highly developed.

The characteristics of the wheel-made ware have been described in connection with the Lung-shan site (Section 40, p. 64), and I shall not repeat them here.

Manchuria and Shantung.—The native wares in Manchuria are hand-made, presumably by ring-building, while the wheel-made ware is somewhat similar to that in Shantung ; the beaten ware with fine impressions of the Lung-shan II type is also found. As in Shantung, the moulded ware is rare.

Of the various methods of pottery-making, there are three chief techniques: (1) hand-modelling, (2) moulding or beating, (3) throwing on the wheel, each of which has its advantages and disadvantages. The modelling method is the easiest technique of all. By coiling, large vessels may be made without much practice. But both modelling and coiling are slow processes, especially so when a definite shape is to be produced. The moulding method is much quicker than hand-modelling. But the shape is often limited by the shape of the mould. The beater method is only suitable for making large vessels : small vessels and accessories of large vessels have to be made separately by other methods. The throwing method is the quickest. Any size or shape can be produced on the wheel. But there is an obvious disadvantage; the wheel technique calls for an expert, its manipulation cannot be learned in a short time.

So far as we can judge from the stratification of known cultural sites in Honan and Shantung and S. Manchuria, the sequence of the three chief methods, from the prehistoric period to the Shang-Yin and Chou, were the following :—

(1) Hand-modelling, including the coiling method; or moulding by means of the string-mould or the hemispherical mould.

(2) Wheel-throwing, and moulding by means of the belt-mould.

(3) Beating with a very rough beater.

(4) Beating with a fine beater, throwing, or throwing and then finishing with the beater.

In Shansi, Shensi, and Kansu the development of methods is as follows :—

(1) As in Honan and Shantung.

(2) Beating with a very rough beater.

(3) Beating with a fine beater, throwing, or throwing and then finishing with the beater.

Surface Treatment

Section 86. Northern and Western Honan.—As regards Red Pottery in Northern Honan, we find a simpler technique of surface treatment than that used in Western Honan. The highly polished shiny surface, which is frequent in Western Honan, is not found in Northern Honan. The application of white slip, or red wash, is rare in Northern Honan; those few specimens from Hsiao T'un and Hou Kang which show such treatment are perhaps imported from Western Honan. The surface of the Black Pottery in Northern Honan is either burnished on the turn-table or on the wheel. Nearly all the grey wares from Honan have an untouched surface, bearing marks either of the mould or the beater. On the inner surface there are either the marks of the hand or the pad.

Honan and Shansi.—The surface of the Red Pottery is just as well prepared in Shansi as it is in Western Honan, and better in Shansi than in Northern Honan ; the red wash and white slip and the highly polished shiny surface are common. It is hardly necessary to mention that there is no such a method as burnishing on the wheel to be found in Shansi and the other provinces west of it. The surface of the coarse wares in Shansi is rougher than that of the Western Honan wares.

The application of slip may have been invented in the process of modelling through the necessity of constantly dipping the clayey hand into water and thereby covering the surface of the pot with a fine silt. The surface of a pot made by ring-building has to be smoothed over with a wet hand in order to fill the crevices. The surface layer thus produced may be called a self-coloured slip. The application of white slip on the Red Pottery is, so far, found only in Western Honan and Shansi ; the purpose is perhaps to imitate the white ware which is rare in the Red Pottery period, and might have been highly valued. The painting of a coat of red colour on the surface must be differentiated from the use of slip ; in the former the red pigment has been used alone without the admixture of any kind of clay, and in the latter the colour is in the clay. In this thesis, I call the coating of colour a wash.

Shansi and Shensi.—The surface of the coarse ware in Shensi is just the same as that of the coarse ware in Shansi, but that of the fine red ware is quite different. No trace of wash or slip has been found in Shensi, and the surface is only slightly polished, far less than is that of the Shansi wares. The coarse wares both from Shansi and Shensi bear string-impressions which do not follow the same invariable parallel arrangement as may be observed on the Honan wares. They are different from the signs of the mould, or beater, in Honan. By a series of experiments, I found that they are impressions of a loose ball of string, which I call a soft beater, the function of which is somewhat similar to that of the coarse beater in Northern Honan. Such impressions, like those on the moulded or beaten wares, are produced in the process of making. With the palm inside, and the soft beater pressing on the outside, the wall of the vessel will be made even, thin, and compact, though not so perfect as that made by the coarse beater and pad.

Shansi, Shensi, and Kansu.—The surface of the Red Pottery in Kansu is smoothed and, if prepared for decoration, polished, but never so highly polished as to acquire a shiny appearance. No white slip and rarely any red wash were used, and only in a few instances was the surface covered with a slip of the same material as the ware itself.

It is of vital importance for us to note the occurrence of beater impressions on some vases from Hsin Tien and Sha Ching, and mould impressions on vases from Ch'i-chia P'ing, all in the Kansu province. On some vases from Turfan in Chinese Turkestan belonging to Professor P. L. Yüan I have noticed beater impressions similar to those on the Kansu vases. This new technique could not have been invented in Kansu or Turkestan, as it appears there in a fully grown stage, while, on the other hand, this technique has passed through several earlier stages of development in Honan. It is quite likely that this technique was introduced into Kansu from Honan, a region with which the ancient Kansu people might have been in contact.

Honan and Shantung.—The surface of the real Black Pottery in Shantung and Honan is highly burnished on the wheel. Polishing with some tool is rarely found in Shantung. The smoothness of the Black Pottery is a characteristic inherited from the Red Pottery period, but the glossy shiny surface is certainly a unique feature. The horizontal string-impressions on the wares from Lung-shan I are similar to the impressions on some red-ware water-jars from Honan.

Manchuria and Shantung.—In comparison with Shantung, the surface of the Manchurian wares is poorly prepared. Smoothing with the wet hand is the usual method of surface treatment in Southern Manchuria. All the beaten wares and some of the wheel-made wares have an untouched surface, and only a few wares are slightly polished.

In all the pottery under discussion, there are two kinds of surface, smooth and rough. Generally speaking, a cooking vessel has a rough surface, while a container has a smooth surface. The methods of producing these surfaces are as follows :—

The smooth surface is produced by smoothing the clay with the wet hand, by polishing, or by burnishing.

The rough surface is produced by moulding, beating, or throwing. The rough surface often possesses some impressions or marks, such as impressions of the mould or basket-work, impressions of matting, beater impressions, roller impressions, and impressions of a single cord rolled over the surface. These impressions may still be divided into two categories, fine and coarse. The purposes of the fine and the coarse impressions are distinct from each other. The fine impressions are often the imprints of a mould or beater covered with fine string, designed merely to prevent the clay from sticking to the instruments ; these fine string-impressions have no particular function, while the coarse impressions are the imprints of a mould or beater covered with coarse string or cord designed to produce a clearly and deeply impressed surface which serves a practical purpose. For instance, the cooking vessel *li* usually has coarse string-impressions and it is interesting to note that sometimes the upper part of it is covered with fine string-impressions, while the feet are covered with coarse string-impressions. In everyday use the top part is farther from the fire while the lower part is always exposed to it. That is why the deep impressions are made here for the purpose of preventing cracking.

From the facts discovered at the excavated sites in Honan, Shantung, and Southern Manchuria we may summarize the sequence of the leading methods of surface treatment, from the Red Pottery period onwards, as follows :—

(1) Polishing by hand with some tool.

(2) Burnishing on the turn-table.

(3) Burnishing on the wheel ; smoothing with the wet hand ; the retention of the untouched surface, consisting of vertical or horizontal string-impressions.

(4) The retention of the untouched surface, and sometimes smoothing in order to prepare it for decoration.

(5) The retention of the untouched surface produced by the fine beater, the wheel or hand techniques, or the trimming of the top part on the wheel.

(6) The retention of the untouched surface produced by the extra-fine beater, and the trimming on the wheel of the top part of the vessel, and the cutting of parallel horizontal lines on the body.

In Shansi, Shensi, and Kansu the changes in methods of surface treatment are as follows :—

(1) As in Honan and Shantung.

(2) Smoothing with the wet hand.

(3) The retention of the untouched surface, and sometimes smoothing in order to prepare it for decoration.

CHAPTER IX

SHAPE

Section 87.—In comparing pottery shapes of the various sites we must pay attention to three things, namely the capacity of the vessel, the number of varieties of shape, and the degree of specialization. Generally speaking, if the capacity is larger, if the number of different shapes is greater, and if the function is more specialized, then the culture is more advanced. Unfortunately the pottery finds under discussion are so fragmentary that many shapes are impossible to identify, and the identified shapes are probably less than one-third of the whole.

Northern and Western Honan.—In Northern Honan, the red and other wares of the Red Pottery period, especially those at Hou Kang, are so simple in shape that there are only about four varieties, *ting*, water-jar, bowls, and basins, which are, as a rule, very small in capacity. These vessels may be divided into two kinds according to their functions, cooking vessels and containers. In Western Honan, the shapes are more varied, and the capacity is larger. Another interesting fact is that the water-jar in Northern Honan has a flat bottom and a small capacity, while in Western Honan its base is pointed, and its capacity large.

Wares of the Black Pottery period of Hou Kang and Hsiao T'un have more than ten different varieties of shape. Their average capacity is found to be about double that of the red ware when two vessels of the same function are compared. The prototype of the *tou* is a product of the Black Pottery period. The common cooking vessels are of two kinds, *ting* and *li*; the *li* found at Hou Kang is the earliest type of *li* known.

Still more advanced in every respect is the grey ware of the

142

Shang-Yin period in Northern Honan ; average sizes are much larger ; shapes are more numerous. Besides the cooking vessels and containers, there are some vessels of beautiful form, and some of the pots from tombs are different from ordinary wares.

Shansi and Honan.—In Shansi the Hsi-yin shapes are similar to those of Yang-shao, but the Ching Ts'un shapes are more varied and the sizes larger. The *ting*, *li*, *yen*, and *tou* are found at Ching Ts'un.

Shensi and Kansu.—In Shensi, basins and bowls are the common shapes. *Ting* and tall-legged *li* and water-jars with a pointed base are also found.

In Kansu there are urns larger than the ordinary Shang-Yin vessels. There are more than twenty different shapes with various kinds of accessory ornaments. *Ting* and *li* are not found in the early periods. Certain globular jars are perhaps intended to be balanced on the head ; they are fundamentally different from the jars with pointed base found in Shansi and Honan.

Shantung and Manchuria.—In Shantung we find the highly developed type of black ware, which is more varied in shape than the same ware in Honan, though the capacity is not much different. During the Black Pottery period in Shantung, *ting*, *yen*, and similar cooking vessels were the characteristic shapes, but there were no *li*.

In Manchuria, from the Sha-kuo T'un pottery finds, the shapes of bowls, deep pots, *li*, and *tou* may be identified. At Tan-T'o Tzŭ and Kao-li Chai, *yen*, *tou*, and other highly specialized shapes are found. The painted pots are objects of ornament.

The main factors that determine the shape are, of course, the function and the technique of manufacture. By function, we can classify the various shapes into three categories, as follows :—(1) cooking vessels : *ting*, *li*, *yen*, etc. ; (2) containers : bowls, basins, jars, etc. ; (3) decorative vessels : ordinary or complicated shapes.

The roundness of pots is produced through experience ; such a shape has its advantages : easy cleaning and immunity from chipping. In storing vessels and water-jars the belly tends to be globular ; while in drinking bowls the mouth is always wide and open. The *min* and *tou* of the Shang-Yin and Chou periods always have a stem. As there was no dining table in the early days, those vessels with a stem would be of a convenient shape on which to serve food to people sitting on a mat or floor.

There is a close relation between the technique of manufacture and the shape. As a result of a special method of making by hand in Kansu, the urns from that place are always globular in shape with the mouth and the base of about the same diameter. In Honan the technique of moulding usually produces a round base, and there is a limit to the varieties of shape which can be made by that method. The wheel technique, as we can see from the black wares in Shantung, has produced most varied and beautiful shapes which can hardly be produced by any other method.

As far as can be judged from our present knowledge, the following are the common shapes in the order of their appearance.

(1) Bowls, basins, water-jars with a flat or pointed base, and *ting* with solid legs.

(2) Large deep basins, the prototype of *tou*, hollow-legged vessels, such as *yen* and similar shapes.

(3) Open pots, deep large water-jars, globular jars, and *li*.

(4) Water-jars with ears and handles, *tou*, and shallow dishes.

(5) Water-jars and basins of enormous capacity.

CHAPTER X

DECORATION

Section 88.—In the Second Part I have mentioned four kinds of decorated wares, viz. painted, incised, pricked, and with applied designs in modelled relief. I am only going to consider painted decoration for purposes of comparison, because it is common to most of the prehistoric sites, though it forms only a small proportion of pottery finds. The incised wares are found in small quantities in Honan and Shantung, and in larger quantities in Manchuria. Their motifs are so simple that they may be included in a single class of simple lineal designs. The pricked ware from Ching Ts'un in Shansi and the wares with designs in relief from Pan-shan and Ssǔ Wa in Kansu are local peculiarities. I shall, therefore, not make any comparison with this scanty material, lest I be led astray by insufficient data.

Western and Northern Honan.—So far as present knowledge goes, the painted decoration of Northern Honan is the simplest type. The pigment used is only one kind which produces a red colour, which is slightly darker than the colour of the ware itself. The painted ware forms a very small proportion of the pottery finds, and its shapes are mostly bowls. The main motifs are bands, lines, vertical or slanting, and triangles. In Western Honan, however, we find that the painted motifs are of an advanced kind, and, with the exception of the triangle, different from those of Northern Honan. The simplest motifs are round spots, triangles, crossed lines ; complicated motifs are made by means of combinations of these elementary motifs, as a rule, symmetrically arranged. The pigments are of two colours, black and red. Painted wares are not only made in the shape of bowls, but also basins, jars, and other shapes.

Shansi and Honan.—In Shansi some of the decorative motifs

(Fig. XXXVIII, 47 and 50) are more complicated than those in Northern Honan, but most of them are similar to those of Yang-shao, though somewhat different from those of Ch'in-wang Chai. The arrangement of the motifs, as in Western Honan, is on a symmetrical basis. Both in Honan and Shansi, the blank spaces between the motifs as well as the motifs themselves were carefully disposed so as to be symmetrical and proportionate. The painting was done on the turn-table.

Shensi and Shansi.—No richly painted ware has been found in Shensi. The only kind of painting is a black band on the rim of bowls and basins, like that which is also found on the same kind of vessels in Shansi.

Kansu and Shensi.—In a very striking way the painted motifs of the Kansu group are different from those of the other groups. The colours are red and black, but the red is seldom so fresh and bright as it is in Western Honan. Except at Hsin Tien, the painting seems to have been done with the intention of covering the surface as much as possible, and not leaving any blank space, contrary to what is found in the Shansi and Honan groups. The shapes of the painted vessels are varied, from small bowls to large urns. The painted decoration, unlike that of the other groups, is intended to be viewed from the top, instead of from the side. The motifs are very complicated, though there are a number of stock designs, which frequently occur. The regularity in the designs is so marked, that I believe the painting was done by mechanical methods. They are executed according to a well established system. There are certain motifs which are characteristic of certain sites such as the tooth pattern of Pan-shan, the medallion of Ma-ch'ang, the double-hook of Hsin Tien, and the animal figures of Sha Ching.

Shantung and Honan.—So far, no trace of the painted ware has been found in Shantung, and the red-coloured ware, which is a suitable medium for the painted designs, is rarely found. The absence of painted ware constitutes the difference between Honan and Shantung wares.

Southern Manchuria, Honan, and Shantung.—The decoration of the four painted sherds from the Sha-kuo T'un Cave shows some similarity to the simplest designs of the Honan group. The technique of these painted sherds is similar to that of the rare red ware of Lung-shan I. The painted sherds from Tan-tʻo Tzǔ have only a few motifs similar to those of the Honan group. Probably the painted ware of Manchuria developed on independent lines with very little influence from the region west of the Great Wall. That is why most of the designs are different from those of Honan.

There are three factors which determine the nature of decoration, symmetry, conservatism, and the quality of the instruments. In ancient as well as modern China the guiding principle of nearly all the designs is symmetry. The simplest kind of design is that based on bilateral symmetry. A bilateral symmetrical motif may stand alone, or may be arranged in a series, according to certain formal schemes. The motifs are comparatively few in number, and they occur again and again without much variation. Each period seems to have had a different but limited repertory. Judging by the curved shapes, the obviously rapid methods of execution, and certain marks of fine hairs, a soft brush and a ball of wool were probably the implements used.

I shall divide all the motifs under discussion into four groups according to their chronological order as follows : in the first group the motifs are elementary such as spots, lines, bands, trellis-work, triangles, and squares, as reproduced on the wares from Hou Kang and Hou-chia Chuang in Northern Honan. In the second group some of the elementary motifs are still retained and new composite motifs are introduced such as those on the wares from Yang-shao Tsʻun and Hsi-yin Tsʻun. At this stage, new types of ornaments such as horizontal furrows, ornamental knobs to the lid, and ears and handles to the body were introduced. In the third group the main motifs are composite such as we may find on the wares from the Kuang-wu district in Western Honan. At this stage incised designs first make their appearance ; they persisted up to the historical period. In the fourth group the motifs are drawn from a limited stock and arranged according to a well-established system, as may be seen on the Pan-shan and Ma-chʻang ware in Kansu, and on the Tan-tʻo Tzǔ ware in Manchuria.

PART IV

THE POTTERY CLASSES

CHAPTER XI

THE SIX CLASSES OF PREHISTORIC POTTERY

Section 89.—After the analytical and comparative studies we come now, as a natural sequence, to the synthetical part of this thesis. I propose to divide the various wares into classes, and then establish a method of describing them concisely. To carry out such a scheme, the only comprehensive method is, of course, to construct a table (see Table 2) to include all the characteristics of pottery, such as colour, material, thickness, etc., which were discussed in Part II. If two colours are equally characteristic of one ware, both of them are entered, and the same rule will apply to material, thickness, method of making, surface treatment, and decoration. I have, however, omitted from the table one characteristic, the shape, as it cannot be described shortly enough. I have not included those sites which still await further investigation, such as Hsin Tien, Ch'i-chia P'ing, Ssŭ Wa, and Sha Ching in Kansu, Fêng-huang T'ai and An-shang Ts'un in Shan-tung. I have taken into account only the well explored and accurately described sites in each group, comprising fifty-seven types of pottery ; a few types are omitted, such as the painted ware from Hsiao T'un and the plain ware from Pan-shan, because they offer too scanty material for study.

Section 90.—Table 2 reveals clearly the fact that the wares fall into six general classes in each of which there may be some slight variations with regard to material or some other characteristics. I call these classes, One, Two, Three, Four, Five, and Six, and I have

TABLE 2

TABULATED SUMMARY OF WARES

Site	Analysis (see Part II)	Colour	Material	Thickness	Method of Making	Surface	Decoration	Class
Hou Kang	Plain Red	Red	Fine	Medium	Hand	Polished	Nil	One
	Plain Black	Black	,,	Thin, Medium	Wheel	Burnished	,,	Two
	Plain Grey	Grey	Coarse	Medium	Hand	Polished	,,	Three
	Decorated	Red	Fine	,,	,,	,,	Painted	One
Hou-chia Chuang	Plain Fine Red	,,	,,	,,	Hand, Mould	,,	Nil	,,
	Plain Fine Black and Grey	Black, Grey	,,	,,	Beater, Hand	Burnished	,,	Two
	Plain Coarse Grey	Grey	Coarse	,,	Hand	Untouched	,,	Three
	Decorated : Painted Red	Red	Fine	,,	Hand, Mould	Polished	Painted	One
	,, Imprinted Black	Black				Burnished	Imprinted	Two
Hsiao T'un	Plain Coarse Grey	Grey	Coarse	Extra Thick	Beater	Untouched	Nil	Three
	Plain Coarse Red	Red		Thick	Mould	Burnished	,,	,,
	Plain Fine Black	Black	Fine	Thin	Wheel	,,	,,	Two
	Plain Fine Grey	Grey	,,	Medium	Beater	Polished, Untouched	,,	,,
	Incised	,,	Coarse	Thick	Mould, Beater		Incised	Three
	White	White	Fine	Medium	,,	Smoothed	Engraved, Nil	Five
Yang-shao	Plain	Grey	Coarse	Thick	Mould	Untouched	Nil	Three
	Decorated	Red	Fine	Medium	Hand	Polished	Painted	One
Pu-chao Chai	Plain	Grey	Coarse	,,	Mould	Untouched	Nil	Three
Ch'in-wang Chai	Plain	Red	Fine	Thin	,,	,,	,,	,,
	Decorated	,,	,,	Medium	Hand	Polished	Painted	One
Ch'ih-kou Chai	Decorated	,,	,,	Thin			Painted	,,
Lung-shan II	Chou Wares, A	Grey	Coarse	Medium	Fine Beater	Untouched	Nil	Three
	,, ,, B	,,	,,	,,	Mould	,,	,,	,,
	,, ,, C	,,	,,	,,	Wheel	,,	,,	,,
Lung-shan I	Plain Coarse (a)	Grey, Black	,,	Thin	Mould	Smoothed	,,	Four
	,, ,, (b)	Grey	Extra Fine	Medium	,,	Untouched	,,	Three
	Plain Fine	Black	Fine	Thin	Wheel	Burnished	,,	Two
	Decorated	,,		,,			Accessories, Incised lines	

Site	Type	Colour	Fineness	Thickness	Technique	Surface	Accessories	Number
Liang-ch'êng	Plain Coarse	Black, Red	Coarse	"	"	Smoothed	Nil	Four
	Plain Fine	Black	Extra Fine	"	"	Burnished	"	Two
	Decorated	"	Fine	"	"	"	Accessories, Incised lines	"
Hsi-yin Ts'un	Plain Coarse	Red, Grey	Coarse	Thick	Hand, Mould	Untouched	Nil	Three
	Plain Fine	Red	Fine	Medium	Hand	Polished	Painted	One
	Decorated	"	"	"				"
Ching Ts'un	Plain Rough	"	"	Thick	Beater, Mould	Untouched	Nil	Three
	Plain Fine	"	"	Medium	Hand, Mould	Polished	Painted, Incised, Pricked	One
	Decorated	"	"	"	"	"		"
Tou-chi T'ai	Plain Coarse	Grey	Coarse	Thick	Mould	Untouched	Nil	Three
	Plain Fine	Red	Fine	Medium	Hand	Smoothed, Polished	"	One
	Decorated	"	"	"	"		Painted	"
Pan-shan	Painted	"	"	"	"	Polished	Painted	"
	Decorated in Relief	Grey	Coarse	Thin	"	Smoothed	Modelled relief	Six
Ma-ch'ang	Painted	Red	Fine	"	"	Polished	Painted	One
Sha-kuo T'un	Plain Coarse	Brown	Coarse	Thick	"	Untouched	Nil	Three
	Plain Fine Red	Red	Fine	Medium	Wheel	Burnished	"	Two
	Plain Fine Black	Black, Grey	"	Thin	Wheel (?)	"	"	"
	Painted	Red	"	Medium	Wheel	"	Painted	"
	Incised	Brown	Coarse	Thick	Hand	Untouched	Incised	Three
	Impressed	"	"	"			Impressed	"
Tan-t'o Tzŭ	Plain Rough	Black	"	"	"	Smoothed	Nil	Four
	Plain Black	"	"	"	Wheel	Polished	Painted	"
	Decorated	"	"	"				"
Kao-li Chai	Plain Black	"	"	"	Hand	Untouched	Nil	"
	Plain Black Gritty	Grey	"	"	Wheel, Beater	Untouched	"	Three
	Plain Grey	Black	"	"	Hand	Polished	Incised	Four
	Decorated	"	"	"				

entered them thus in the last column of that table. These six classes are described in the following table :—

TABLE 3

THE SIX CLASSES OF PREHISTORIC POTTERY

Class	Colour	Material	Thickness	Technique	Surface	Decoration	Shape
One	red	fine	medium	hand-modelled	polished	with or without painted designs	bowls, basins, jars.
Two	black	fine	thin	wheel-made	burnished	plain	bowls, basins, jars, *ting*, beakers with ears and handles.
Three	grey	coarse	thick	moulded	untouched	plain	water-jars with pointed or round base, open pots, deep water-jars, *tou, min, li,* and other bronze shapes.
Four	brown or black	coarse	thick	wheel-made	smoothed	plain or decorated	*yen,* and other hollow-legged vessels.
Five	white	fine	thick	beaten	smoothed	plain or decorated	*min.*
Six	grey	coarse	thin	hand-modelled	smoothed	modelled in relief	deep jars.

Chapter XII

DISTRIBUTION OF THE SIX CLASSES

Section 91.—From Table 2 we may see that the pottery classes of the various sites are as follows :—

TABLE 4

Classes	Provinces	Sites
One	Honan	Ch'ih-kou Chai
	Kansu	Ma-ch'ang
One, Two, and Three	Honan	Hou Kang Hou-chia Chuang
One and Three	Honan	Yang-shao Ch'in-wang Chai
	Shansi	Hsi-yin Ts'un Ching Ts'un
	Shensi	Tou-chi T'ai
One and Six	Kansu	Pan-shan
Two and Three	S. Manchuria	Sha-kuo T'un
Two, Three, and Four	Shantung	Lung-shan
Two and Four	Shantung	Liang-ch'êng
Two, Three, and Five	Honan	Hsiao T'un
Three and Four	S. Manchuria	Kao-li Chai
Three	Honan	Pu-chao Chai
Four	S. Manchuria	Tan-t'o Tzŭ

From the above data, and from the descriptions in Part I and Part II, the geographical distribution of the various classes can be traced. Class One has a wide distribution nearly all over the Plateau. Up to the present, not a single piece of Class One ware has yet been discovered in Shantung. The eastern boundary of its distribution seems to coincide with the boundary of the primary loess (roughly indicated by the P'ing-Han Railway). Only a small proportion of Class One is highly ornamented with painted designs. This painted ware has an uneven distribution; in Northern Honan it is comparatively rare, while in Western Honan and Shansi it is frequent. As far as we can tell at present, it was, however, the chief class of ware in Kansu, where it is superior in every way to the painted ware in any other place.

So far as I am aware, no Black Pottery culture was established in the Plateau area, where Class Three directly succeeded Class One. After the end of the Black Pottery period in the Plain, Class One still persisted to a time as late as the beginning of the Chou dynasty.

Class Two seems to cover the whole Great Plain, and its influence also penetrated as far as the Huai Valley and Hang-chou Bay. I have noticed a few Black Pottery sherds among the pottery finds from Hsi-yin in Southern Shansi (Section 97, p. 167), a region which was probably in constant communication with Western Honan in ancient times.

The ware of Class Three covers practically the whole area treated in this thesis, i.e. North China. In the historic period, its influence has extended into Manchuria and Mongolia, and a large part of South China. How far south it has reached is still a question. Class Four is found in Shantung and Manchuria. It is rare in Honan. Class Five is not uncommonly found at Hsiao T'un in Northern Honan. Its earlier stages have, however, covered a much wider area: Shansi, Honan, and Shantung. At present, Class Six has only been found at Pan-shan in Kansu. To sum up, let us show the distribution of the Six Classes in the following map (Map II).

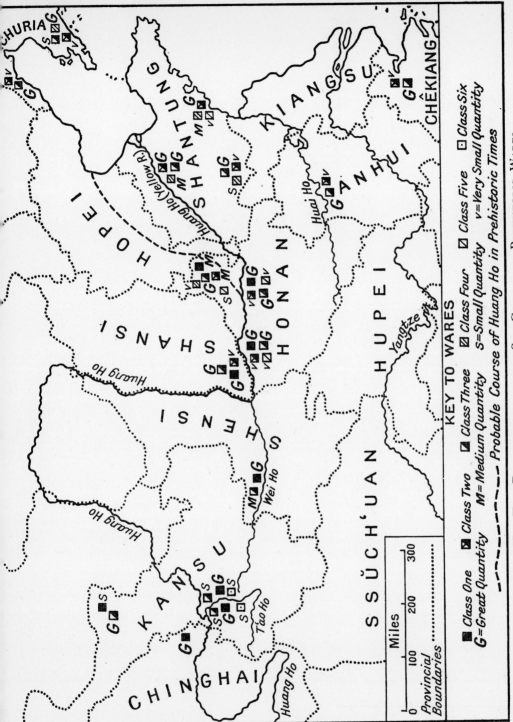

MAP II. THE DISTRIBUTION OF THE SIX CLASSES OF PREHISTORIC WARES.

Chapter XIII

POINTS OF RESEMBLANCE AND DISTINCTIVE PECULIARITIES OF THE WARES IN THE SIX CLASSES

Section 92.—Both the wares of Classes One and Two are made of fine material. This similarity may be explained by the fact that fine clay in the loess area of North China can easily be procured from natural sources, and prepared through simple washing processes. The extra-fine material of Class Two is, however, characteristic of the Black Pottery period, as no such fine material has ever been used either before or since. The method of preparing this fine clay is levigation which is an improvement on the washing method of the Red Pottery period. The employment of such fine material is due to the demand for thin-walled vessels ; the finer the material the thinner the wall can be made.

Class One is, to a certain extent, peculiar in two respects, the red colour and the painted designs. That is why it is sometimes called the Red Pottery or the Painted Pottery. The peculiarities of Class Two are the black colour, the wheel-technique, and the burnished surface. It is usually called the Black Pottery.

Class Three was rare in the Red Pottery period. It was made in greater quantities in the Black Pottery period. There is hardly any similarity between the Classes One and Three. There is one feature shared by the Classes Two and Three : except in some extremely rare instances, neither class is painted with pigment, and the surface is usually plain ; if there is any decoration at all, it is often executed either by treating the surface itself, or by adding ornaments on to the surface. In ornamentation, Class Three is inferior to Class Two. Ears and knobs on the wares of Class Two serving as ornaments are rarely used in this way on Class Three. We find ears and knobs on Class Three wares but they are intended for purely practical purposes.

The most striking feature of Class Three is the rough surface with mould or beater marks, due to which the ware is sometimes called the string-impressed, or mat-marked ware.

Both Classes Two and Four are black in colour, but the black of Class Four is usually lighter and less uniform in tone than that of Class Two. Both are wheel made. We should not expect to find these two classes in the region west of the present boundary of Shansi province, because the wheel was not used there till the historic period. The peculiarity of Class Four is the coarseness of the material. In Shantung, Class Four and Class Two are found together, and Class Four also shows a high standard of wheel technique. I believe that these two classes, Two and Four, in Shantung, might have been made by the same potters, and baked together in the same kiln.

The peculiarity of Class Five is the white colour. In Shansi and Western Honan where it has been found together with Class One, it is similar to that class in technique, while in Shantung where it is found together with Class Two, it is similar to the wheel-made coarse ware, Class Four ; and at Hsiao T'un it is similar to the ware of Class Three. Therefore, we may say that Class Five has a development closely parallel to that of the four classes, One, Two, Three, and Four.

Class Six is grey in colour and of coarse material like Class Three ; it has a thin wall like Class Two, it is hand-made like Class One, and it has the smoothed surface like Class Four and Class Five. The modelled relief is its own peculiarity.

PART V

CHRONOLOGY AND SUMMARY

M

CHAPTER XIV

THE CHRONOLOGICAL SEQUENCE OF THE PREHISTORIC SITES

Section 93.—In dealing with the provincial groups in the Second Part, I have arranged the sites of each group in a chronological order, which is based on the evidence of stratification and pottery types. The present theme is to construct a chronological sequence of the prehistoric sites in China (Table 5) by putting side by side all the provincial sites in their chronological order and so to discover in what relation each site stands to all others in point of time. The Table is merely an attempt at relative, not absolute, dating, and it is not to be regarded as conclusive. The method that I shall adopt is to compare the pottery of adjacent regions in the following respects : (1) the presence of the same type, or class, of pottery ; (2) the presence of pottery with certain characteristics in common ; (3) the evidence afforded by associated finds. I shall treat the adjacent regions in the following order :—

(1) Western Honan in reference to Northern Honan.
(2) Shantung in reference to Northern Honan.
(3) Southern Manchuria in reference to Shantung and Honan.
(4) Shansi in reference to Honan and Shantung.
(5) Shensi in reference to Shansi.
(6) Kansu in reference to Shensi, Shansi, and Honan.

Section 94. WESTERN HONAN IN REFERENCE TO NORTHERN HONAN.—Judging by the simple shapes, simple motifs, and the absence of white slip and polychrome painting on the sherds from the proper Red Pottery layer at Hou Kang I, Hou-chia Chuang I, and Ta-lai Tien I, one would naturally come to the conclusion that the Red Pottery of Northern Honan, except the Liu Chuang site, should be earlier in date than that from Western Honan. (Mr. S. Y. Liang was the first to point out this fact. See his article, Bibl. 20.)

It cannot be inferred that this group of painted pottery represents a period of degeneration, because it has simpler shapes and more primitive technique than the Western Honan ware. The degeneration of a highly developed ceramic art can only follow the introduction of another art, which serves the original purpose better, or the invention of a new technique. Neither alternative can be proved, because in the associated objects of the same layer we can find no indication either of a new art, such as bronze-casting, or of a new technique, such as the potter's wheel. One should not argue that this group in Northern Honan was an outlying manifestation of the painted pottery culture with its centre at Kansu. Take, for example, two sites to illustrate this point. Tan-t'o Tzŭ site in Southern Manchuria is farther away from Kansu than Western Honan, but painted pottery with complicated designs is found there. Tou-chi T'ai in Shensi is nearer to Kansu than Western Honan ; but the designs on its painted pottery are much simpler than those of Western Honan. My opinion is that the Northern Honan Group represents an early stage (certainly earlier than Yang-shao) of the painted pottery. The comparatively small proportion of painted pots among the Red wares may be explained by the fact that ornamentation was not widely practised at that time. No objects other than pottery are decorated. The bowl was the vessel most commonly used in everyday life for eating and drinking, and it was the first to be decorated. Even in modern China, the bowls and dishes for food, rather than the washing utensils, are those that bear designs.

In Western Honan the only site where the early type of Red Pottery occurs is T'a P'o. Its technique is similar to the red ware of Ta-lai Tien in Northern Honan, but its decorative motifs are more complicated.

Among the finds from Yang-shao I have noticed certain pots made according to the Black Pottery technique (Fig. LVIII–LIX). It is clear that the beaker (Fig. LIV) is a typical Lung-shan shape, and is wheel-made, being polished to the same degree as the Lung-shan wares. The bowl (Fig. LV) is also made according to the Lung-shan technique ; it is dark brownish-grey, but the outside, near the margin, has been polished to look like black lacquer. Fig. LVIII is like a Lung-shan basin (Fig. LVI) in shape and technique, and Fig. LIX is a vessel of reddish brown colour with a black shiny surface, also made according to the Lung-shan technique. There is one complete specimen of a coarse grey-ware *ting* (Fig. LX) of Lung-shan technique and shape. Legs of this type of vessel were found in large quantities at the Lung-shan site (Bibl. 31, Pl. XIII, 13). A peculiar form, such as this, applied to the body in the same way as it is at Lung-shan, could hardly have been evolved independently. It is unlikely that these characteristics are local products ; probably they were derived from the area of the Black Pottery culture. So far as I can see, the coarse ware (Class Three) of Yang-shao is similar in technique to that of Hsin Ts'un and Ta-lai Tien II, and I venture to say that the top layer of Yang-shao may be contemporary, i.e. dating from the decline of the Black Pottery culture. To the same period belongs Pu-chao Chai, where coarse ware (Class Three) is found similar to that of Hsin Ts'un, not only in technique but also in shapes. The beaten ware with squares on the surface is found both at Pu-chao Chai (Fig. LXI) and at Hsin Ts'un, and the tall-legged *li* is found at both places.

Section 95. SHANTUNG IN REFERENCE TO NORTHERN HONAN.—The Black Pottery (Class Two), either the typical or the pseudo-black, from Lung-shan and Liang-ch'êng in Shantung is so similar to that from Hou Kang II and Hsiao T'un I that these two groups are hardly distinguishable from each other. The peculiar shapes of the Black Pottery period, such as the *ting*, and the hollow-legged vessels with their peculiar accessories, are also similar in these two regions. Besides pottery, there are at Hou Kang and at Lung-shan the same types of oracle bones, stone and shell and bone implements. The similarity between the artifacts of Hou Kang and Lung-shan existed in ancient times and it exists to-day. It is reasonable to suppose that these two ancient sites are contemporaneous.

The An-shang Ts'un and Fêng-huang T'ai sites in Shantung

represent a later stage of the Black Pottery culture. A parallel stage is found in Honan at the sites Hsin Ts'un and Ta-lai Tien II. In this stage when the Black Pottery technique declined and the output decreased both in Honan and in Shantung, the coarse ware increased enormously. The coarse wares of An-shang Ts'un or Fêng-huang T'ai, and Hsin Ts'un or Ta-lai Tien are very similar to each other. That is the main reason why I put them in the same period.

The cultural layer of the second period of Lung-shan belongs to a historic period. Its pottery is similar to that of Hou-chia Chuang III, but it has some advanced features : shapes are more varied, the beater is much finer, and the wheel was evidently more widely used. That is why I put it later than Hou-chia Chuang III.

Section 96. SOUTHERN MANCHURIA IN REFERENCE TO SHANTUNG AND HONAN.—I have already mentioned the Chinese influence on Manchurian culture in my remarks on Sha-kuo T'un, Tan-t'o Tzǔ, and Kao-li Chai, and also the reason why I think Sha-kuo T'un II is contemporary with the Shang-Yin, and Sha-kuo T'un III–VI with Eastern Chou (Section 74, p. 115). It is clear that the Black Pottery technique influenced the wheel-made ware (Class Two), and the red painted ware from Sha-kuo T'un I. The earliest date of this deposit is therefore about the same as Lung-shan I.

The latest date of the Manchurian group is fixed by the discovery of Chinese pottery and Chinese coins at Kao-li Chai in the second layer. As has been proved, its date may be as late as the Han (Section 79, p. 121), and therefore it is the latest type of ware discussed in this thesis, even later than Lung-shan II, the last period of which is probably the seventh century B.C. (Section 41, p. 66).

Section 97. SHANSI IN REFERENCE TO HONAN AND SHANTUNG.—We are indebted to the careful methods of the excavator, Dr. Li Chi, for his accurate records which make it possible to estimate the date of the Hsi-yin site. The exact position of every object excavated and its associated materials have been set on record. Among the finds from layer A (Square 5) between the depths 0·76–0·93 m., I noticed four pieces of *li* sherds of the Hsiao T'un type, i.e. the surface of which is covered with deep and fine string-impressions. I established the fact that they did not belong to one and the same vessel. It can hardly be argued that they were brought there during the Shang-Yin period for the purpose of burial, as no burial pits, human bones, or any other funerary objects were discovered. These four sherds were found in three different depths (0·76, 0·86, and 0·93 m.). If they were put there at the same moment, we should expect to find them together at the same depth. Nor can one argue that they were local products, because, as we have already mentioned, no *li* or *ting* or any other three-footed cooking vessels were made at Hsi-Yin. The only explanation is, therefore, that these *li* sherds were transported from the Shang-Yin domain during the last period (layer A) of Hsi-Yin. In other words, this period was contemporary with the Shang-Yin. As no other material later than Shang-Yin was found in the top layer (layer A), I think this site must have been abandoned in that period.

As the layer B is below layer A, it must be earlier than the Shang-Yin. Among the finds from layer B, I noticed more than thirty sherds of black ware. They are not the real Lung-shan type, but they are thin, about 5 mm. on the average, with a polished surface, but not as shiny as Lung-shan ware. The outer surface is black while the inner is grey. In short, they represent the pseudo-black ware of the Black Pottery period in Northern Honan. I also noticed a type of bowl-shaped lid of gritty ware (Fig. LXII) which was used both to cover cooking vessels and as a container during the Black Pottery period ; in addition a lid with a bird's head to serve as a knob-handle, which is exactly the same as that found at Lung-shan I, and at Liang-ch'êng (Fig. XXXV, *f*). I found only one handle of a jug (Fig. LXIII) and one leg of a *ting*, but they are the types characteristic of the Black Pottery period. Summing up all the foregoing evidence, I think layer B (third period) is of the same period as the fully developed stage of the Black Pottery culture in Honan and Shantung.

Taking pottery Class One as the main criterion, the first and second periods (layer C and D) of Hsi-yin Ts'un may be dated as contemporary with Yang-shao I and Ch'in-wang Chai respectively.

Their shapes are similar, and so is their technique, especially the highly polished surface, and the use of white slip. The simple decorative motifs of Hsi-yin are similar to those of Yang-shao I, while the complicated ones are similar to those of Ch'in-wang Chai.

Section 98. SHENSI IN REFERENCE TO SHANSI.—Oh the whole, the plain wares Classes One and Three of Tou-chi T'ai in Shensi are very similar to those of Hsi-yin Ts'un in Shansi. But there is a difference to be noted in the decorated ware, i.e. the decoration is far simpler, and surface treatment less careful than the corresponding features of the ware found at Hsi-yin. Further, the *li* is common at Tou-chi T'ai, whereas only a few *li* sherds are found in the top layer of Hsi-Yin Ts'un. Judging by those facts, I believe that the date of Tou-chi T'ai should be later than Hsi-Yin by a short period.

Section 99. KANSU IN REFERENCE TO SHENSI, SHANSI, AND HONAN.—A similar type of plain coarse ware like that of Pu-chao Chai (Class Three) was found at Ch'i-chia P'ing, and the early type of *li* was found at Ssŭ Wa. The painted ware, Class One, at Pan-shan and Ma-ch'ang is of a technique similar to the painted ware found in Shensi, Shansi, and Honan. But there is one apparent difference, that is the painted designs are not only more complicated but also more advanced as regards methods of execution, than any of those which have been found in Shensi, Shansi, or in Honan. Some of the Kansu motifs are more like those of Tan-t'o Tzŭ in Manchuria than those from Shensi, Shansi, or Honan. In my opinion the date of Pan-shan and Ma-ch'ang is contemporary with the last two periods of Shansi and Shensi. Furthermore there are two facts that I wish to mention, not as another evidence, but as tests of my dating. (1) The Pan-shan urns are especially made for burials : in other words, they are *ming ch'i*. So far as I know from modern discoveries, *ming ch'i* were rarely used during the Shang-Yin period, when real objects of daily use were deposited in the tomb ; they were used more often in the Chou, but not till the Han were they common. Their date can hardly be earlier than Hsiao T'un II, when the custom of using *ming-ch'i* was known but not fully established. (2) Both the Pan-shan and the Ma-ch'ang vases seem to have a wide distribution

168

in Kansu, and some of them have potters' marks. There is little room for doubt that they were commercial articles. As modern discoveries have revealed, potters' marks, and even owners' marks, rarely appear on pottery before the Shang-Yin (Bibl. 31, pp. 53–54, on marks of the Chou period). In the Chou period when pottery became an ordinary article of commerce, potters' marks were frequent. As the potters' marks on the Kansu vases cannot serve any other purpose than that of advertising the artisan, it must be admitted that those vases were made at a time when economic conditions were the same as in the Chou period.

The Hsin Tien and Sha Ching vessels bear marks of the fine beater (Figs. LXV and LXVI). Wares made by means of the early type of beater are found at Hsiao T'un II (Fig. LXIV), but the products of the fully developed type of beater are to be found at the sites of the Chou period in Honan and Shantung. The best examples are the Chou wares of Lung-shan II (Fig. LXVII). As there is in Honan and Shantung a continuous development of the fine beater technique it cannot be argued that this technique had been invented in Kansu and suddenly appeared as a mature craft. So we should expect the date of Hsin Tien and Sha Ching not to be earlier than Lung-shan II. Furthermore, the discovery in the Sha Ching tombs of cowries and turquoise beads (Bibl. 3, p. 18), which are often found in Chou, but rarely in later tombs, seems to point to the same fact. Dr. Andersson says in his article, *Der Weg über die Steppen* (Bibl. 4, p. 153), that the date of Sha Ching should be about 600–100 B.C. on the basis of the discovery of bronzes of the so-called Scythian type together with the painted pottery. This is certainly an interesting suggestion though I doubt the possibility of dating the Sha Ching, or any other pottery, by Scythian bronzes, the origin and development of which are still obscure.

TABLE 5

CHRONOLOGICAL SEQUENCE OF PREHISTORIC SITES
Including Sites where Prehistoric Wares Persisted into Historic Times. (Sites entered on the same line are contemporary.)

S. Manchuria	Shantung	Northern Honan	Western Honan	Shansi	Shensi	Kansu
		Hou Kang I Hou-chia Chuang I Ta-lai Tien I				
		Liu Chuang	T'a P'o			
			Yang-shao I	Hsi-yin I		
		Hou-chia Chuang II	Ch'in-wang Chai Ch'ih-kou Chai Ch'en Kou	Hsi-yin II		
		Hou Kang II Hsiao T'un I	Ch'ing T'ai	Hsi-yin III		
Tan-t'o Tzǔ Sha-kuo T'un I	Lung-shan I Liang-ch'éng					
	Fêng-huang T'ai An-shang Ts'un	Hsin Ts'un Ta-lai Tien II	Yang-shao II Pu-chao Chai			Ch'i-chia P'ing
At the sites below this line certain prehistoric wares persisted into historic times.						
Sha-kuo T'un II		Hou Kang III Hsiao T'un II		Hsi-yin IV Ching Ts'un I		Pan-shan
Kao-li Chai I Sha-kuo T'un III–VI				Ching Ts'un II	Tou-chi T'ai	Ma-ch'ang
		Hou-chia Chuang III Ta-lai Tien III				
						Ssǔ Wa
						Hsin Tien
	Lung-shan II					Sha Ching
Kao-li Chai II						

CHAPTER XV

SUMMARY

Section 100.—The aim of this thesis in five parts is to make a systematic study of prehistoric pottery in China in order to formulate a chronological sequence of prehistoric sites.

Part I describes the scope of the study and the methods used, and sums up the results of recent discoveries of ancient sites.

Part II contains the description and analysis of the pottery finds included in seven provincial groups : Northern Honan, Western Honan, Shantung, Shansi, Shensi, Kansu, and Southern Manchuria. The studies are based on seven selected characteristics, namely colour, shape, material, thickness, technique, surface, and decoration. An account is given of the various early techniques peculiar to China, such as the methods of moulding and beating and of trimming on the turn-table, or burnishing on the wheel. None of these techniques has hitherto been properly explained.

As a result of this analysis it is made possible to arrange the various sites in each provincial group in a chronological sequence.

In Part III comparisons are made between the provincial groups. All the provinces west of Honan are found to share similar characteristics in prehistoric periods, such as the red colour, the medium thickness of the wall, the polishing of the surface, the hand-modelling technique, and the painting of designs. Honan and Shantung have shared, since the Black Pottery period, similar characteristics, such as the black colour, the thinness of the wall, the wheel-technique, the burnishing of the surface, and the absence of decoration. Southern Manchuria has certain characteristics, such as the black colour and the wheel-technique, similar to those of Honan and Shantung since the Black Pottery period. The conclusion reached from these comparisons

171

is that each characteristic underwent a certain change in a certain order of time.

Part IV is a summary of the descriptive and comparative studies (Part II and Part III) leading up to a division of all the prehistoric wares into six classes.

Part V explains the chronological sequence of the prehistoric sites, based mainly on the results of my study of pottery.

SELECTED BIBLIOGRAPHY

1. ANDERSSON, J. G. *An Early Chinese Culture.* Article in *Bulletin of the Geological Survey of China*, No. 5, part i (1923), pp. 1–68.
2. —— *The Cave Deposit at Sha-kuo T'un in Fengtien.* *Palæontologia Sinica*, series D, vol. i, fascicle i. Peking : 1923.
3. —— *Preliminary Report on Archæological Research in Kansu.* *Memoirs of the Geological Survey of China*, series A, No. 5. Peking : 1925.
4. —— *Der Weg über die Steppen.* Article in *Bulletin of the Museum of Far Eastern Antiquities*, Stockholm, No. 1 (1929), pp. 143–163.
5. —— *Children of the Yellow Earth.* London : 1934.
6. ARNE, T. J. *Painted Stone Age Pottery from the Province of Honan, China.* *Palæontologia Sinica*, series D, vol. i, fascicle 2. Peking : 1925.
7. BLACK, D. *The Human Skeletal Remains from the Sha-Kuo T'un Cave Deposit in Comparison with those from Yang-shao Tsun and with recent North China Skeletal Material.* *Palæontologia Sinica*, series D, vol. i, fascicle 3. Peking : 1925.
8. FRANKFORT, H. *Studies in Early Pottery of the Near East.* Two parts. London : 1924 and 1927.
9. HAMADA, K. *P'i-tzu-wo, prehistoric Sites by the River Pi-liu Ho, South Manchuria.* Tokyo : 1929.
10. KUO PAO-CHÜN. *Honan ku chi yen chiu hui ch'êng li san chou nien kung tso k'ai k'uang* (河南古蹟研究會成立三周年工作概况). K'ai-fêng : 1935.
11. —— *T'ao ch'i* (陶器). Article in *Ch'êng-tzŭ-yai* (1934), pp. 55–72.
12. LI CHI. *Archæological Survey of the Fên River Valley, Southern Shansi, China.* Article in *Smithsonian Miscellaneous Collections*, vol. lxxviii, No. 7 (1927), pp. 123–137.
13. —— *Hsi-yin Ts'un shih ch'ien ti i ts'un* (西陰村史前的遺存). Shanghai : 1927.
14. —— *Hsiao T'un yü Yang-shao* (小屯與仰韶). Article in *Preliminary Reports of Excavations at An-yang*, Part ii (1929), pp. 333–348.
15. —— *Ch'êng-tzŭ Yai fa chüeh ti li yu chi ch'i ch'êng chi* (城子崖發掘的理由及其成績). Chi-nan : 1930.
16. —— *Fu shên tsang* (俯身葬). Article in *Preliminary Reports of Excavations at An-yang*, Part iii (1931), pp. 447–480.
17. LI CHING-TAN. *Shou Hsien Ch'u mu tiao ch'a pao kao* (壽縣楚墓調查報告). Article in *T'ien yeh k'ao ku pao kao*, No. 1 (1936), pp. 213–279,
18. LIANG SSŬ-YUNG. *New Stone Age Pottery from the Prehistoric Site at Hsi-yin Ts'un, Shansi, China.* Menasha, Wis. : 1930.
19. —— *Hou Kang fa chüeh hsiao chi* (後岡發掘小記). Article in *Preliminary Reports of Excavations at An-yang*, Part iv (1933), pp. 609–625.
20. —— *Hsiao T'un, Lung-shan yü Yang-shao* (小屯龍山與仰韶). Article in *Studies Presented to Ts'ai Yuan-p'ei on his Sixty-fifth Birthday*, Part ii (1935), pp. 555–565.

173

21. LIU YAO. *Honan Hsün Hsien Ta-lai Tien shih ch'ien i chih* (河南濬縣大賚店史前遺址). Article in *T'ien yeh k'ao ku pao kao*, No. 1 (1936), pp. 69–89.

22. LIU YÜ-HSIA. *Yin tai yeh t'ung shu chih yen chiu* (殷代冶銅術之研究). Article in *Preliminary Reports of Excavations at An-yang*, Part iv (1933), pp. 681-696.

23. LUCAS, A. *Ancient Egyptian Materials and Industries.* London: 1934.

24. PALMGREN, N. *Kansu Mortuary Urns of the Pan Shan and Ma Chang Groups Palæontologia Sinica*, series D, vol. iii, fascicle 1. Peip'ing: 1934.

25. SHIH CHANG-JU. *Ti ch'i tz'ŭ Yin-hsü fa chüeh E ch'ü kung tso pao kao* (第七次殷虛發掘E區工作報告). Article in *Preliminary Reports of Excavations at An-yang*, Part iv (1933), pp. 709-728.

26. SUNG YING-HSING. *T'ien kung k'ai wu* (天工開物). Osaka: 1833.

27. TUNG KUANG-CHUNG. *Shansi Wan-ch'üan shih ch'i shih tai i chih fa chüeh chih ching kuo* (山西萬泉石器時代遺址發掘之經過). Article in *Shih ta yüeh k'an* (師大月刊), No. iii (1923), pp. 99-111.

28. UMEHARA, S. *Etude sur la Poterie Blanche Fouillée dans la Ruine de l'Ancienne Capitale des Yin.* Kyôto: 1932.

29. WU, G. D. *P'ing-ling fang ku chi* (平陵訪古記). Article in *Bulletin of the National Research Institute of History and Philology*, vol. i, part vi (1930), pp. 471-486.

30. —— *Ch'êng-tzŭ Yai ti ts'êng chih kou ch'êng* (城子崖地層之構成). Article in *Ch'êng-tzŭ-yai* (1934), pp. 11-25.

31. —— *T'ao p'ien* (陶片). Article in *Ch'êng-tzŭ-yai* (1934), pp. 36-54.

32. —— *Kao ching t'ai tzŭ san chung t'ao yeh k'ai lun* (高井臺子三種陶業概論). Article in *T'ien yeh k'ao ku pao kao*, No. 1 (1936), pp. 201-211.

33. WU, G. D., and LIANG, S. Y. *Chien chu chih i liu* (建築之遺留). Article in *Ch'êng-tzŭ-yai* (1934), pp. 26-35.

34. —— *Shih ku chio pêng chi chin shu chih ch'i* (石骨角蚌及金屬製器). Article in *Ch'êng-tzŭ-yai* (1934), pp. 73-89.

INDEX

ILLUSTRATIONS

N.B.—In the following pages the black ink represents black in all its various tones. Red pigment is expressed by means of small black spots. The red ground colour and the red wash are not shown at all. The short broken lines in Fig. LIIb mean yellow pigment.

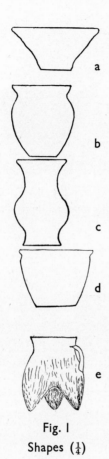

Fig. I
Shapes ($\frac{1}{4}$)

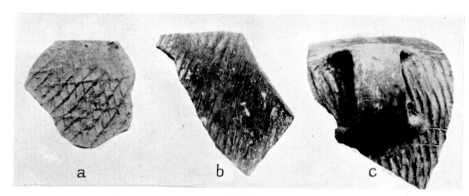

Fig. II
Grey Ware with imprinted marks ($\frac{1}{3}$)

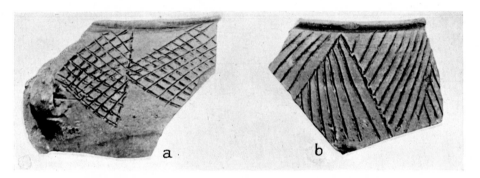

Fig. III
Incised Ware ($\frac{1}{3}$)

2

Fig. IV

Ting and types of *ting* legs ($\frac{1}{3}$)

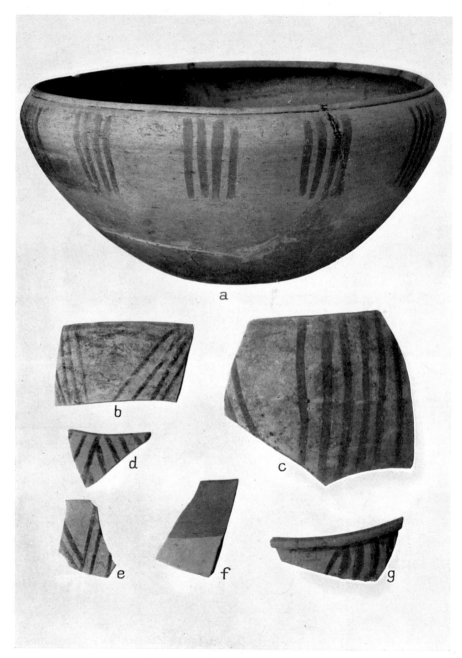

Fig. V
Painted Ware ($\frac{1}{3}$)

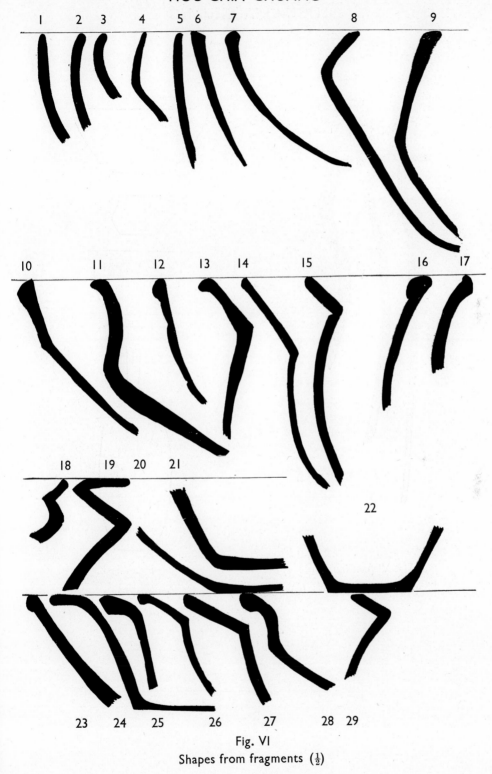

Fig. VI

Shapes from fragments ($\frac{1}{2}$)

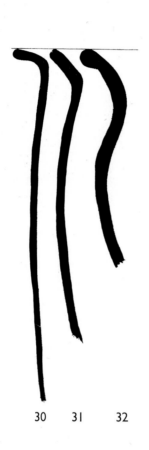

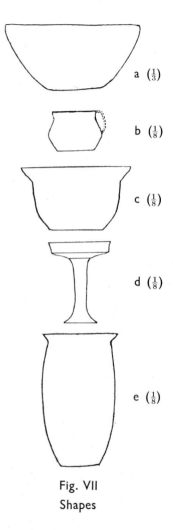

a $(\frac{1}{3})$

b $(\frac{1}{8})$

c $(\frac{1}{8})$

d $(\frac{1}{8})$

e $(\frac{1}{8})$

30   31   32

Fig. VI *(continued)*
Shapes from fragments $(\frac{1}{2})$

Fig. VII
Shapes

Fig. VIII

Sherd with vertical string-impressions $(\frac{1}{2})$

Fig. IX

Sherd with vertical string-impressions $(\frac{1}{2})$

Fig. X

Painted Ware $(\frac{4}{7})$

Fig. XI

Painted Ware ($\frac{1}{2}$)

Fig. XII

Painted Ware ($\frac{1}{2}$)

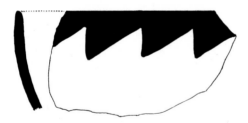

Fig. XIII

Painted Ware ($\frac{1}{2}$)

Fig. XIV

Painted Ware ($\frac{1}{2}$)

Fig. XV
Painted Ware ($\frac{1}{2}$)

Fig. XVIa
Imprinted Ware ($\frac{1}{2}$)

Fig. XVIb
Imprinted Ware ($\frac{1}{2}$)

Fig. XVII
Water-jar with impressions of the beater ($\frac{1}{2}$)

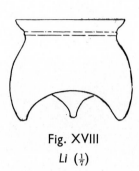

Fig. XVIII
Li ($\frac{1}{7}$)

Fig. XIX
" Helmet " ($\frac{1}{7}$)

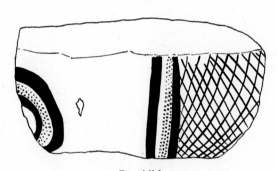

Fig. XX
Painted Ware ($\frac{1}{2}$)

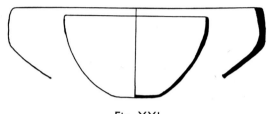

Fig. XXI
Shapes ($\frac{1}{6}$)

Fig. XXII
Shapes from fragments ($\frac{1}{6}$)

Fig. XXIII
Painted Ware ($\frac{1}{2}$)

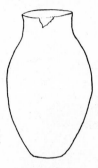

Fig. XXIV

Water-jar ($\frac{1}{8}$)

Fig. XXV

Water-jar ($\frac{1}{10}$)

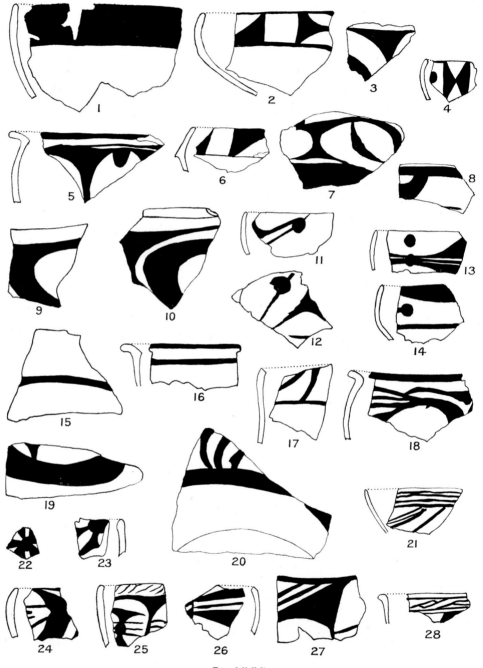

Fig. XXVI

Painted Ware ($\frac{1}{4}$)

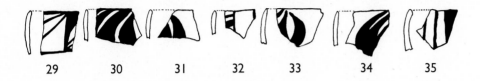

29   30   31   32   33   34   35

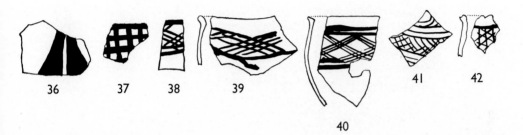

36   37   38   39   40   41   42

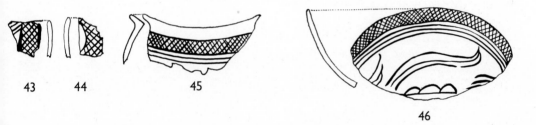

43   44   45   46

47

Fig. XXVI *(continued)*
Painted Ware ($\frac{1}{4}$)

15

Fig. XXVII
Water-jar ($\frac{1}{4}$)

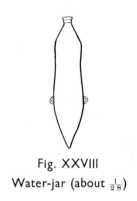

Fig. XXVIII
Water-jar (about $\frac{1}{28}$)

16

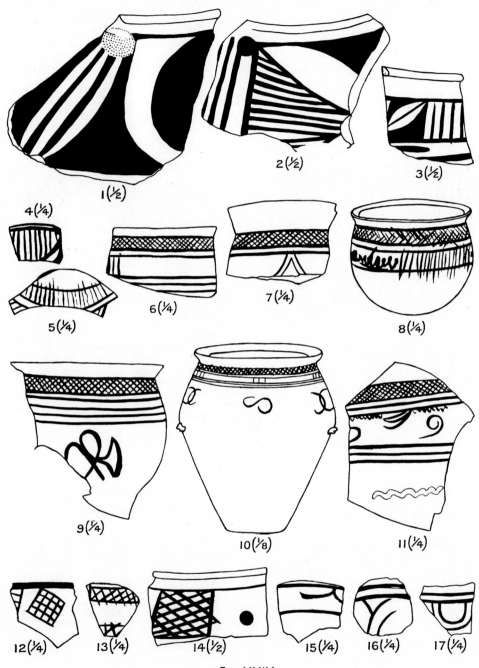

Fig. XXIX
Painted Ware

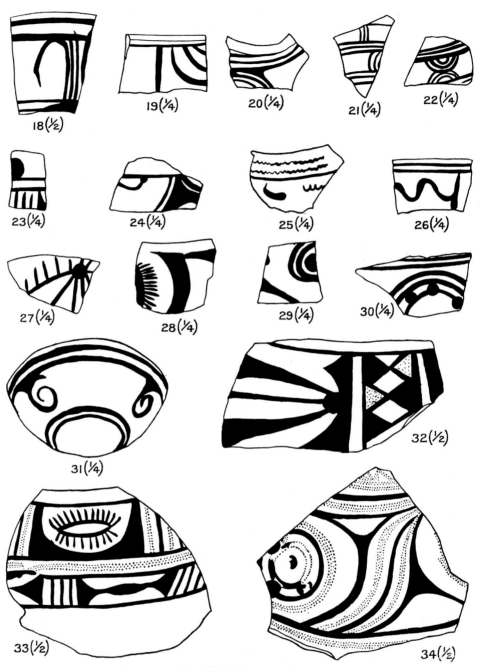

18(½)

19(¼)   20(¼)   21(¼)   22(¼)

23(¼)   24(¼)   25(¼)   26(¼)

27(¼)   28(¼)   29(¼)   30(¼)

31(¼)   32(½)

33(½)   34(½)

Fig. XXIX (continued)
Painted Ware

1 ($\frac{1}{6}$)

2 ($\frac{1}{4}$)

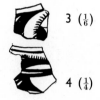

3 ($\frac{1}{6}$)

4 ($\frac{1}{4}$)

5 ($\frac{1}{8}$)

Fig. XXX
Painted Ware

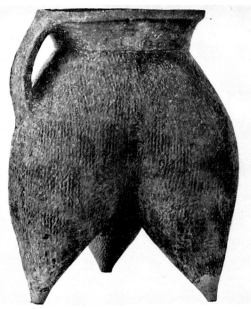

Fig. XXXI
Li (about $\frac{1}{3}$)

Fig. XXXII
The upper part of the *Yen* ($\frac{1}{4}$)

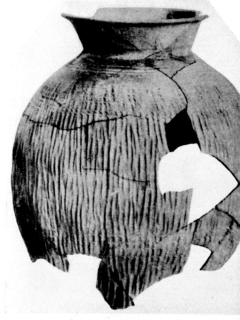

Fig. XXXIII
Pot with regular striae on the rim and the neck

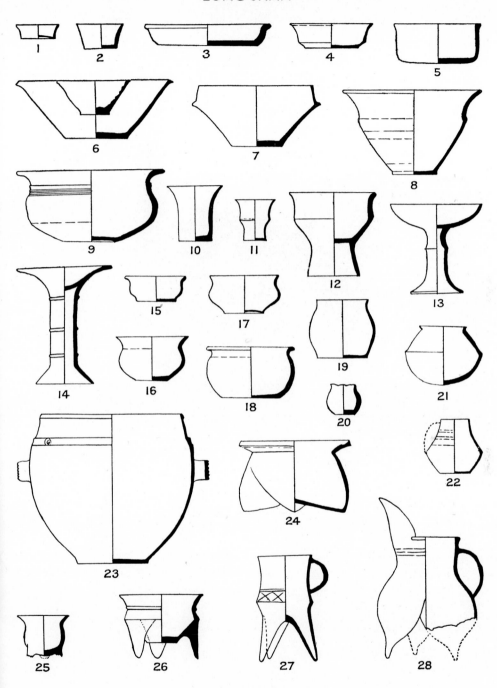

Fig. XXXIV
Shapes ($\frac{1}{7}$)

Fig. XXXV
Wheel-made Pot ($\frac{1}{2}$)

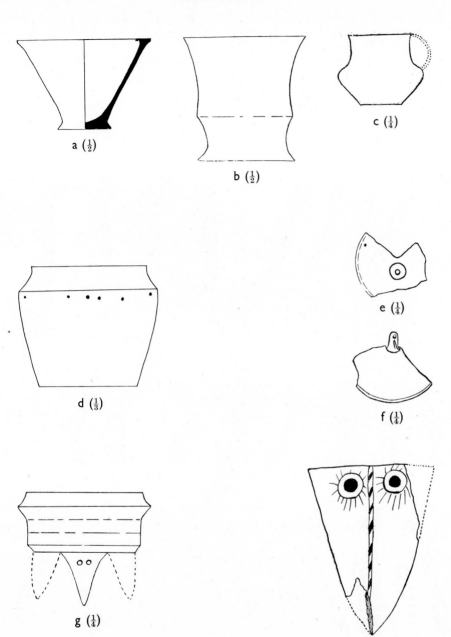

a $(\frac{1}{2})$

b $(\frac{1}{2})$

c $(\frac{1}{4})$

d $(\frac{1}{3})$

e $(\frac{1}{4})$

f $(\frac{1}{4})$

g $(\frac{1}{4})$

h $(\frac{1}{3})$

Fig. XXXVI
Shapes

23

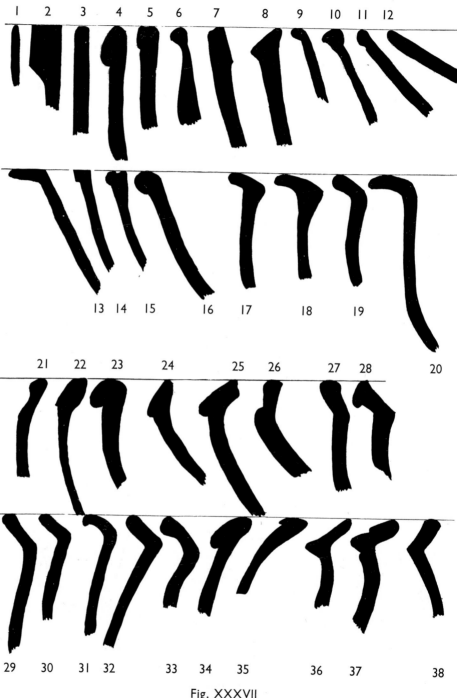

Fig. XXXVII

Shapes from fragments ($\frac{1}{2}$)

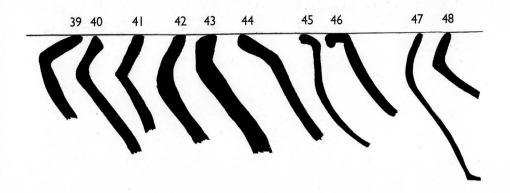

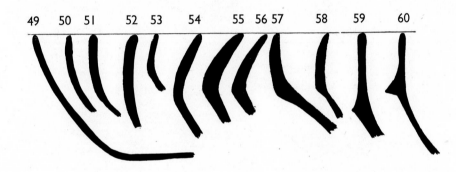

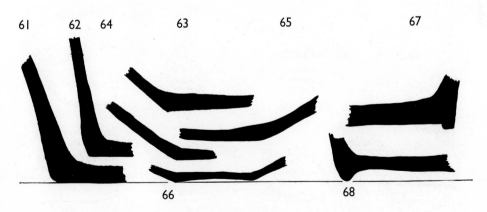

Fig. XXXVII *(continued)*
Shapes from fragments ($\frac{1}{2}$)

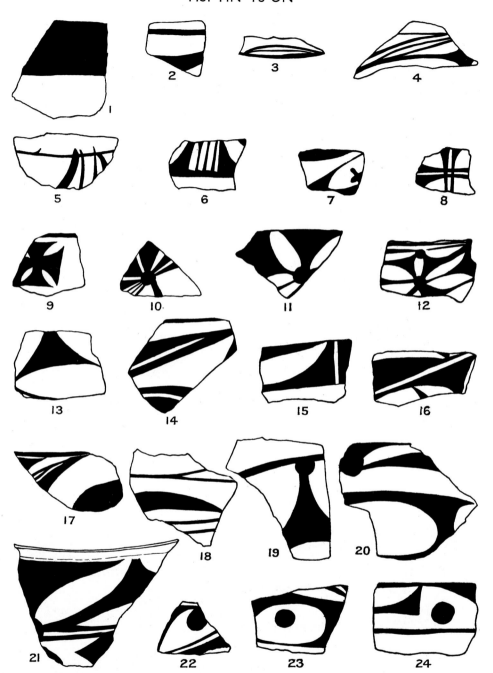

Fig. XXXVIII
Painted Ware ($\frac{1}{3}$)

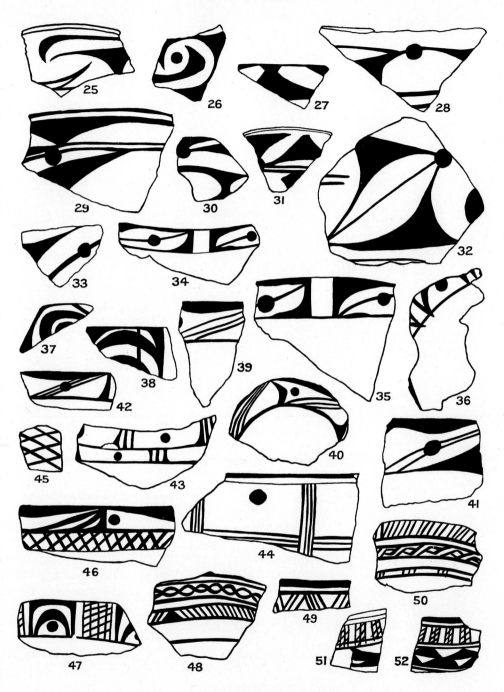

Fig. XXXVIII *(continued)*
Painted Ware $(\frac{1}{3})$

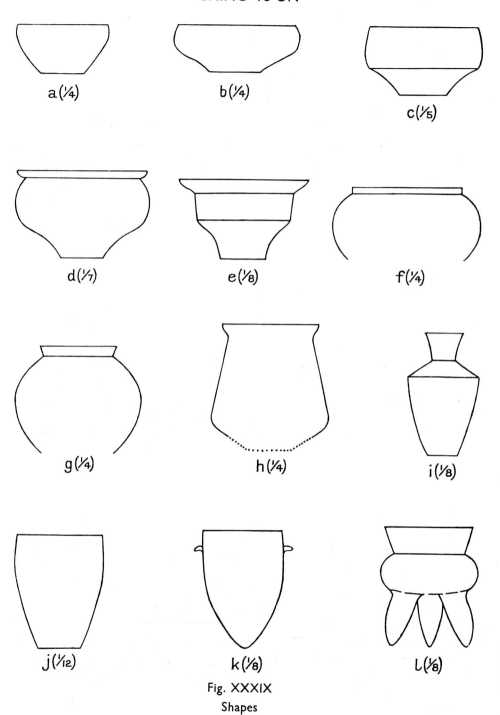

a(¼) b(¼) c(⅕)

d(⅐) e(⅛) f(¼)

g(¼) h(¼) i(⅛)

j(¹⁄₁₂) k(⅛) L(⅛)

Fig. XXXIX
Shapes

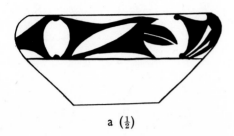

a (½)

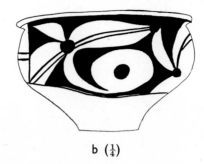

b (¼)

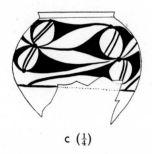

c (¼)

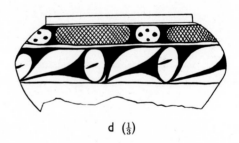

d (⅓)

Fig. XL
Painted Ware

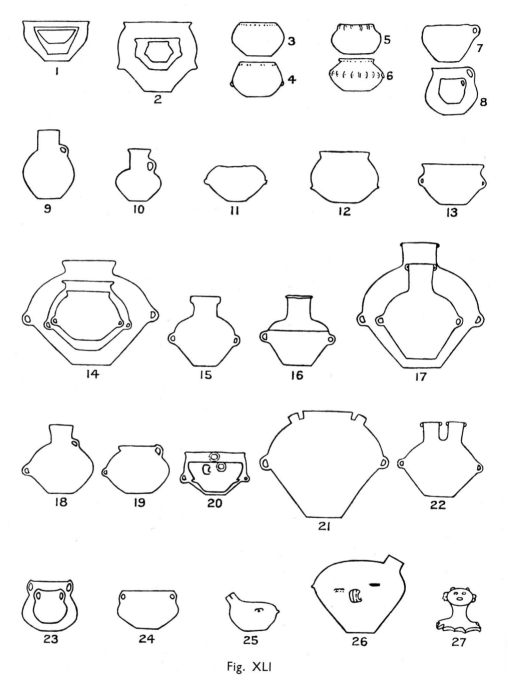

Fig. XLI

Shapes (about $\frac{1}{12}$)

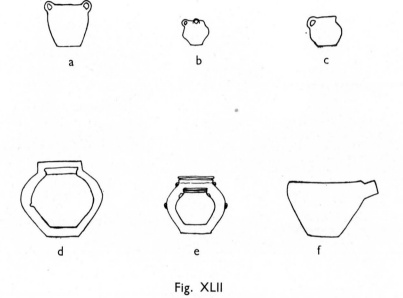

Fig. XLII
Shapes (about $\frac{1}{12}$)

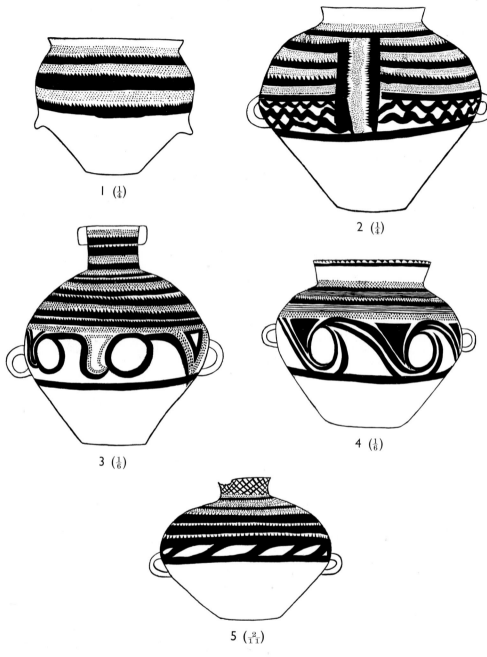

1 $(\frac{1}{4})$

2 $(\frac{1}{4})$

3 $(\frac{1}{6})$

4 $(\frac{1}{6})$

5 $(\frac{2}{11})$

Fig. XLIII
Painted Ware

6 ($\frac{1}{6}$)

7 ($\frac{1}{9}$)

8 ($\frac{1}{9}$)

9 ($\frac{1}{6}$)

10 ($\frac{1}{6}$)

11 ($\frac{1}{1\frac{1}{2}}$)

Fig. XLIII (continued)
Painted Ware

12 ($\frac{1}{9}$)

13 ($\frac{1}{9}$)

14 ($\frac{1}{8}$)

15 ($\frac{1}{6}$)

16 ($\frac{1}{4}$)

17 ($\frac{1}{7}$)

Fig. XLIII *(continued)*
Painted Ware

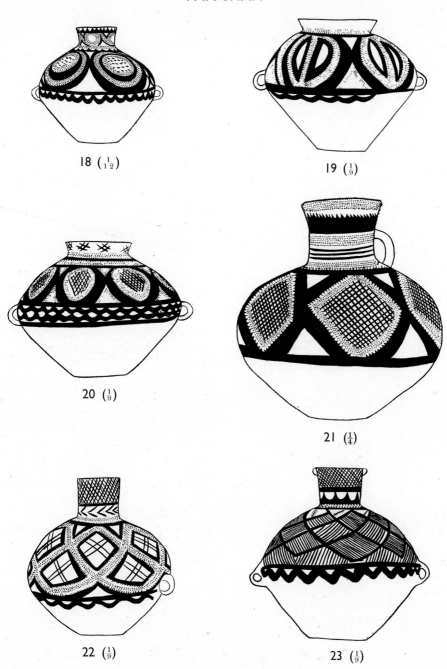

18 ($1\frac{1}{2}$)

19 ($\frac{1}{9}$)

20 ($\frac{1}{9}$)

21 ($\frac{1}{4}$)

22 ($\frac{1}{9}$)

23 ($\frac{1}{9}$)

Fig. XLIII *(continued)*
Painted Ware

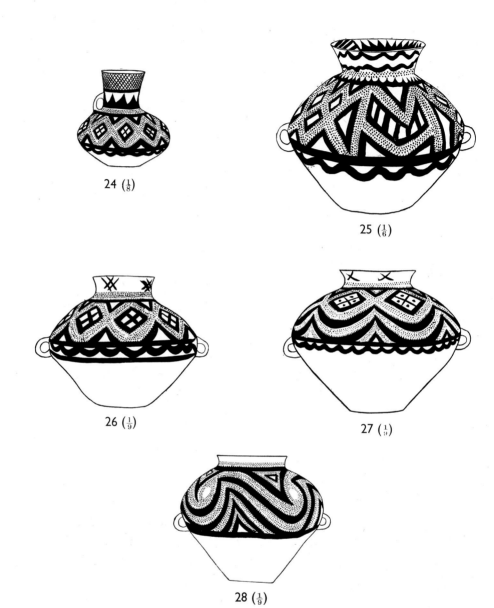

24 ($\frac{1}{8}$)

25 ($\frac{1}{6}$)

26 ($\frac{1}{9}$)

27 ($\frac{1}{9}$)

28 ($\frac{1}{9}$)

Fig. XLIII *(continued)*
Painted Ware

29 $(\frac{1}{10})$

30 $(\frac{1}{12})$

31 $(\frac{1}{12})$

32 $(\frac{1}{9})$

33 $(\frac{1}{12})$

34 $(\frac{1}{7})$

Fig. XLIII (continued)
Painted Ware

PAN-SHAN

35 ($\frac{1}{8}$)

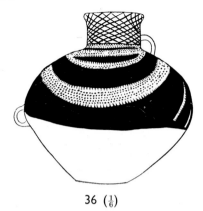

36 ($\frac{1}{6}$)

37 ($\frac{1}{12}$)

38 ($\frac{1}{6}$)

39 ($\frac{1}{6}$)

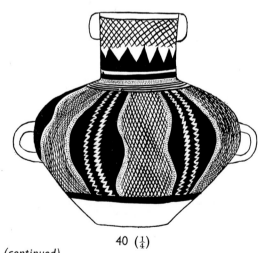

40 ($\frac{1}{4}$)

Fig. XLIII (continued)
Painted Ware

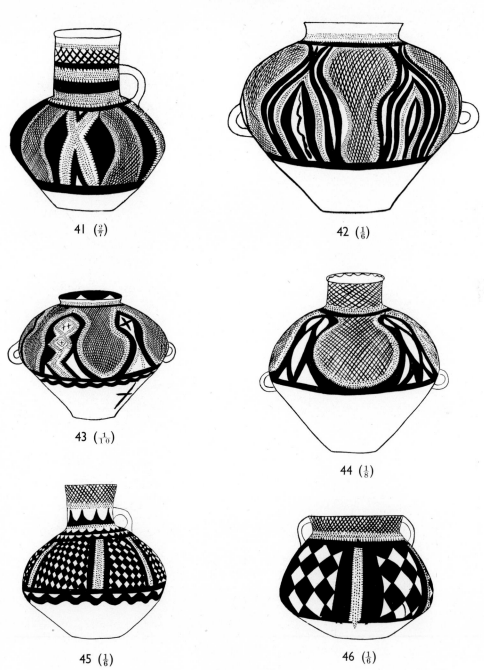

41 $(\frac{2}{7})$

42 $(\frac{1}{6})$

43 $(\frac{1}{10})$

44 $(\frac{1}{8})$

45 $(\frac{1}{6})$

46 $(\frac{1}{6})$

Fig. XLIII *(continued)*
Painted Ware

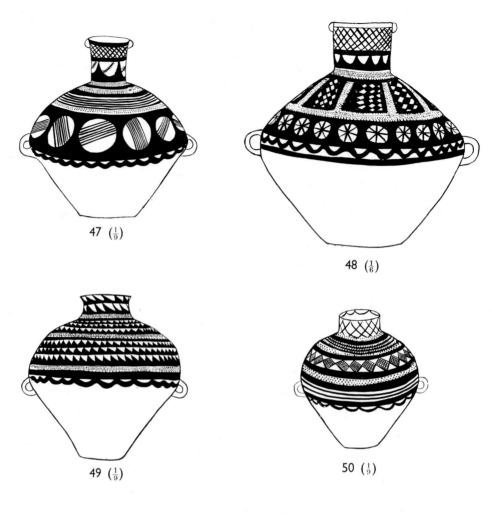

47 ($\frac{1}{9}$)

48 ($\frac{1}{6}$)

49 ($\frac{1}{9}$)

50 ($\frac{1}{9}$)

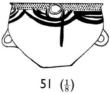

51 ($\frac{1}{8}$)

Fig. XLIII *(continued)*
Painted Ware

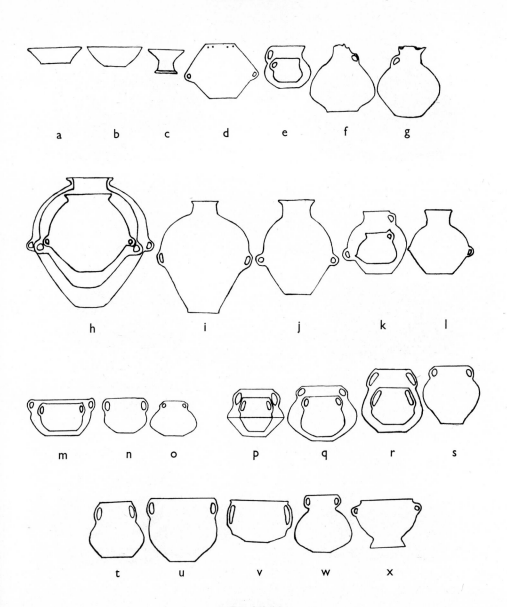

a   b   c   d   e   f   g

h   i   j   k   l

m   n   o   p   q   r   s

t   u   v   w   x

Fig. XLIV
Shapes (about $\frac{1}{12}$)

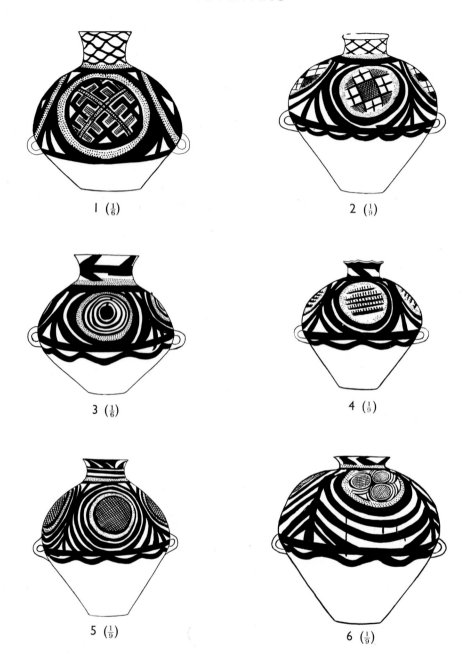

1 ($\frac{1}{6}$)

2 ($\frac{1}{9}$)

3 ($\frac{1}{6}$)

4 ($\frac{1}{9}$)

5 ($\frac{1}{9}$)

6 ($\frac{1}{9}$)

Fig. XLV
Painted Ware

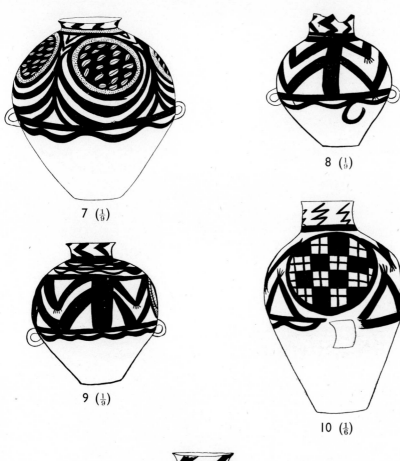

7 ($\frac{1}{9}$)

8 ($\frac{1}{9}$)

9 ($\frac{1}{9}$)

10 ($\frac{1}{6}$)

11 ($\frac{1}{6}$)

Fig. XLV (continued)
Painted Ware

43

12 ($\frac{3}{8}$)

13 ($\frac{1}{4}$)

14 ($\frac{1}{3}$)

15 ($\frac{1}{3}$)

16 ($\frac{1}{6}$)

17 ($\frac{1}{9}$)

Fig. XLV (continued)
Painted Ware

18 ($\frac{1}{4}$)

19 ($\frac{1}{4}$)

20 ($\frac{1}{6}$)

21 ($\frac{1}{8}$)

22 ($\frac{1}{6}$)

23 ($\frac{1}{4}$)

Fig. XLV *(continued)*
Painted Ware

24 ($\frac{1}{3}$)

25 ($\frac{1}{4}$)

26 ($\frac{1}{4}$)

27 ($\frac{1}{4}$)

28 ($\frac{1}{4}$)

29 ($\frac{1}{4}$)

Fig. XLV *(continued)*
Painted Ware

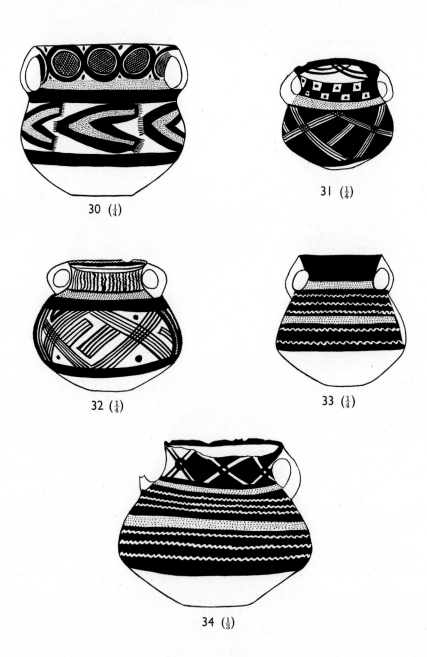

30 ($\frac{1}{4}$)

31 ($\frac{1}{4}$)

32 ($\frac{1}{4}$)

33 ($\frac{1}{4}$)

34 ($\frac{1}{3}$)

Fig. XLV *(continued)*
Painted Ware

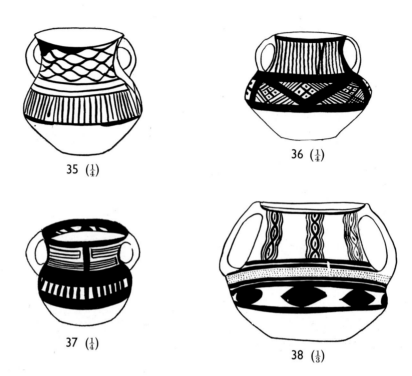

35 ($\frac{1}{4}$)

36 ($\frac{1}{4}$)

37 ($\frac{1}{4}$)

38 ($\frac{1}{3}$)

39 ($\frac{1}{4}$)

Fig. XLV (*continued*)
Painted Ware

40 ($\frac{1}{3}$)

41 ($\frac{1}{9}$)

42 ($\frac{1}{4}$)

43 ($\frac{1}{4}$)

44 ($\frac{1}{4}$)

45 ($\frac{1}{4}$)

Fig. XLV (continued)
Painted Ware

46 ($\frac{1}{6}$)

47 ($\frac{1}{9}$)

48 ($\frac{1}{5}$)

49 ($\frac{1}{5}$)

50 ($\frac{1}{5}$)

Fig. XLV *(continued)*
Painted Ware

Fig. XLVI
Painted Ware ($\frac{2}{9}$)

Fig. XLVIIa
A pot of Plain Fine Ware ($\frac{1}{2}$)

Fig. XLVIIb
Sherd with comb impressions ($\frac{1}{1}$)

a ($\frac{1}{2}$)

b ($\frac{3}{4}$)

Fig. XLVIII

Painted Ware

Fig. XLIX
Ssŭ Wa Ware

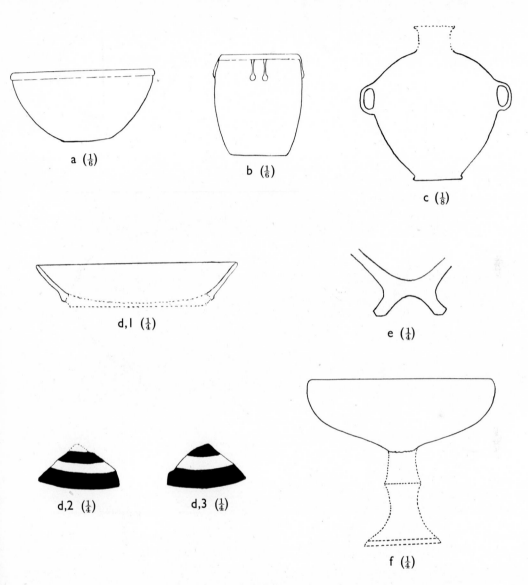

a $(\frac{1}{6})$

b $(\frac{1}{6})$

c $(\frac{1}{8})$

d,l $(\frac{1}{4})$

e $(\frac{1}{4})$

d,2 $(\frac{1}{4})$

d,3 $(\frac{1}{4})$

f $(\frac{1}{4})$

Fig. L
Shapes.   Only d has a painted design

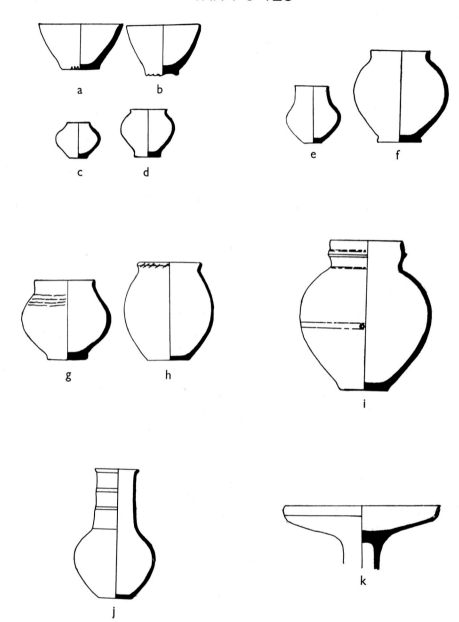

Fig. LI
Shapes ($\frac{1}{6}$)

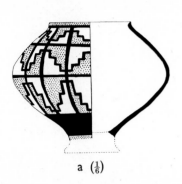

a ($\frac{1}{6}$)

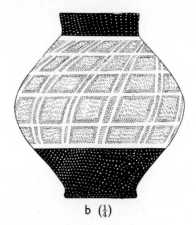

b ($\frac{1}{4}$)

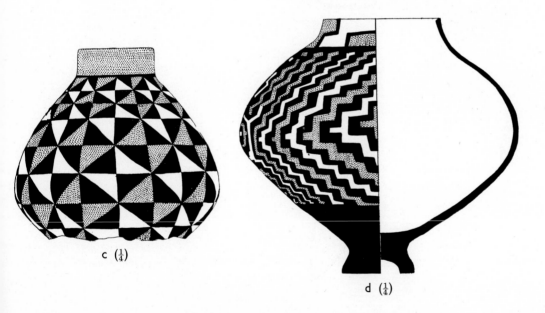

c ($\frac{1}{4}$)

d ($\frac{1}{4}$)

Fig. LII
Painted Ware

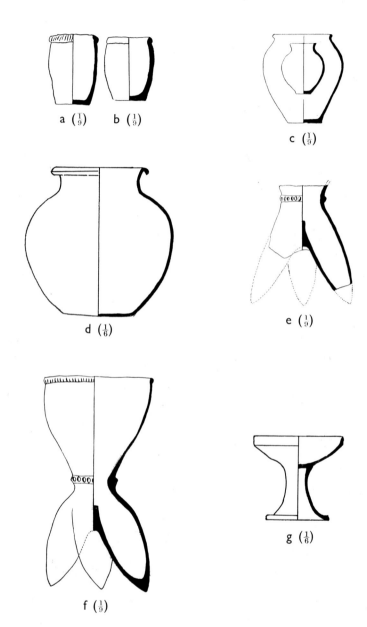

a $\left(\frac{1}{9}\right)$ b $\left(\frac{1}{9}\right)$

c $\left(\frac{1}{9}\right)$

d $\left(\frac{1}{6}\right)$

e $\left(\frac{1}{9}\right)$

f $\left(\frac{1}{9}\right)$

g $\left(\frac{1}{6}\right)$

Fig. LIII
Shapes

Fig. LIV
A Yang-shao beaker ($\frac{1}{5}$)

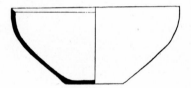

Fig. LV
A Yang-shao bowl ($\frac{1}{5}$)

59

Fig. LVI
A Lung-shan basin (about ⅔)

Fig. LVII
A vessel from Yang-shao, the bowl of which sho[ws]
clear signs of wheel technique (¼)

Fig. LVIII
A Yang-shao basin (¼)

Fig. LIX
Yang-shao black ware (¼)

Fig. LX
A Yang-shao *ting* (about ⅓)

Fig. LXI
Beaten ware from Pu-chao Chai (¼)

Fig. LXII

A Hsi-yin bowl, which was also used as a lid ($\frac{1}{4}$)

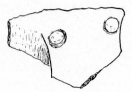

Fig. LXIII

Part of a jug handle from Hsi-yin ($\frac{1}{2}$)

Fig. LXIV
Pot with beater marks from from Hsiao T'un ($\frac{1}{3}$)

Fig. LXV

Pot with beater marks from Hsin Tien (about $\frac{1}{3}$)

(By courtesy of Messrs. Ernest Benn, Ltd.)

Fig. XLVI

Pot with beater marks from Sha Ching

Fig. LXVII

Pot with beater marks from Lung-shan II (about $\frac{1}{3}$)